The Gun

A "Biography" of the Gun
That Killed John F. Kennedy
Henry S. Bloomgarden

Grossman Publishers
A Division of The Viking Press
New York, 1975

First published in 1975 by Grossman Publishers
625 Madison Avenue, New York, N.Y. 10022

Published simultaneously in Canada by
The Macmillan Company of Canada Limited

Printed in U.S.A.

Library of Congress Cataloging in Publication Data

Bloomgarden, Henry S.
  The gun : a "biography" of the gun that killed John F. Kennedy.
  1. Firearms—Laws and regulation—United States. 2. Firearms indus-
try and trade—Terni, Italy (City) I. Title.
HV8059.B55   363.3′3   75-4702
ISBN 0-670-35763-4

Acknowledgments:
Charles Scribner's Sons: "I Have a Rendezvous with Death" from
Poems by Alan Seeger (Copyright 1916 Charles Scribner's Sons).

The Society of Authors on behalf of the Bernard Shaw Estate:
Excerpt from *Major Barbara*.

For Craig and Kirk
and
to Italy—warm, generous, beautiful

Acknowledgments

I am grateful for the help and encouragement given me by many people during the time I researched and wrote this book. But a small number get my especial thanks: Karen Kriendler Nelson, who has studied and lived in Italy, and suggested people who would initially be helpful once I arrived there; Sid Goldberg, Editor of North American Newspaper Alliance, for general support from the time I first showed him the eight-page outline that started all of it; Matty Rosenhaus and Jerry Cossman, who helped me get to Italy and gave me understanding after I returned; Irving Kristol, who took time to read a first draft and made perceptive suggestions; Daniel Okrent, my editor, who took this on and gave it so very much; John Hawkins, my agent, who always had faith; John Kalkbrenner, my translator in Italy; Lydia Dal Dosso, my translator in the United States; Gerry Van Der Heuvel, at the American Embassy in Rome; James Walker, at the National Archives in Washington; Carol Rinzler, who read the manuscript and recommended I take it to Dan Okrent for publication.

Contents

"I Have a Rendezvous with Death"

I have a rendezvous with Death
At some disputed barricade,
When Spring comes back with rustling shade
And apple-blossoms fill the air—
I have a rendezvous with Death
When Spring brings back blue days and fair.

It may be he shall take my hand
And lead me into his dark land
And close my eyes and quench my breath—
It may be I shall pass him still.
I have a rendezvous with Death
On some scarred slope of battered hill
When Spring comes round again this year
And the first meadow-flowers appear.

God knows 'twere better to be deep
Pillowed in silk and scented down,
Where Love throbs out in blissful sleep,
Pulse nigh to pulse, and breath to breath,
Where hushed awakenings are dear . . .
But I've a rendezvous with Death
At midnight in some flaming town,
When Spring trips north again this year,
And I to my pledged word am true,
I shall not fail that rendezvous.

—Alan Seeger

Prologue

It was a spring Sunday in 1963, with glorious weather and a breeze fragrant with magnolia blossoms, countless flower beds, and carefully cut grass. The President had worked the morning and now wanted to stretch his legs beyond the Oval Office. His family was away for the weekend.

He thought of his close friend Charles Bartlett, at whose home he had first met Jacqueline Bouvier. He picked up the telephone: "Charlie, let's get out for a walk."

Bartlett and the President went to the Air and Space Museum on Independence Avenue and stayed a while inspecting various exhibits and talking about nothing in particular, nothing monumental.

Outside the museum they were undecided where to go next. Still uncertain, they entered a waiting limousine. Bartlett does not recall whether it was he or the President who suddenly said, "Let's go over to Arlington."

They drove to the Custis-Lee Mansion, where Robert E. Lee had married Mary Custis, great-granddaughter of George Washington's wife, and where Lee had decided in the spring of 1861 to cast his lot with the Confederacy.

There, beneath the pillars of the portico, high on the hillside of the Arlington National Cemetery, Bartlett and the President were silent for a number of minutes, savoring the profound restfulness of the graveyard where tens of thousands of servicemen are buried. From this vantage point they could look down over the few remaining unused acres, toward the city of Washington, across the Potomac. It was in a mood of calm, brought on by the abiding quiet and the view, that the President said, somewhat jovially, as though to make light of the pomp of office and the pace and weight of its responsibility, "You know, maybe we should move the White House up here."

The President and Bartlett spent an hour walking among the grave markers nearby, reading inscriptions about men who had served their country—commodores, admirals, generals, captains, enlisted men, now, at last, companions all. They talked little. There was solemnity, inspired by a deep sense of history.

Near the end of the hour spent among the graves, Bartlett and the President climbed back toward the Custis-Lee Mansion. They turned to look at the sea of undulating slopes, at the green grass flecked by a flotilla of white crosses in eternal formation. Bartlett asked the President, "Are you going to be buried here?" The President shook his head unknowingly. "I suppose I ought to go back to Boston," he said.

Then the President took a deep breath and sighed, "But, Charlie . . . I could stay here forever."

Sandy Richardson thought it *was* forever. He lay on the Italian hillside thinking he was dead, then gradually realized he was only wounded. His helmet had been taken off and his scalp creased by a German sniper's bullet. His head bleeding, he was running down the slope, seeking safety, and had kicked a land mine with his foot. It had tossed him in the air with its explosive force. It should have blown him to shreds. If he hadn't been stumbling downhill, falling forward, it might have. Instead, he had a broken back and a broken leg.

Unable to move, he lay there while another GI kept calling for a medic. At last, after eight hours, some "very beautiful guys" came along with a jeep, placed him on a stretcher, lifted him off the hillside to the hood, and took him to a field hospital.

During some of the eight long hours, Private Sandy

Richardson heard the sound of German 88s, 120 mortars, American M1s, and Mannlicher-Carcanos. The Carcano was used by Italian partisans fighting there, alongside the Americans, in the mountains near Pian d'Ontani, in the province of Pistoia, far north of Rome. This was the third time Richardson had been conscious of the peculiar sound of these rifles.

Weeks earlier he had seen other partisans unearth a cache of Carcanos and decide that day to settle old scores. Collaborators were taken from their homes and shot.

Then there was the time the partisans, armed with Carcanos, accompanied Richardson's outfit on patrol, early one morning, before first light. Richardson heard the sound of the M1s shooting at the Germans, ". . . a loud 'chunk,' solid, definitely there." In contrast, the Carcano, with its smaller bore and seemingly underpowered cartridges, sounded "much like a firecracker. . . . I couldn't believe they were serious. . . . I thought the bullets would poop out and drop harmlessly . . . no trajectory . . . it sounded like the Fourth of July."

Three times, then, he had heard the Carcanos. The day the collaborators were shot. The morning on patrol with the partisans. And the day—April 9, 1945—he was shot and blown up and lay on the hillside while the battle went on. Fifteen and more years later he still could hear the firecracker sound.

⊕

On November 22, 1963, Sandy Richardson, then vice-president of a publishing company, was having lunch with Richard Johnston, executive editor of *Sports Illustrated*, in the restaurant atop the Time-Life Building in New York City. The waiter came to the table, quietly, almost apologetically, very unsure: "Mr. Johnston, I beg your pardon. The President has been assassinated."

"What!"

"In Dallas."

They left the table and went to Johnston's office. In the hours that followed, Richardson was stunned not just by the news, but by reports from people on the scene. Some believed the shots had been automobile backfire. Some said they had sounded like firecrackers. And Richardson, hearing this, remembered, and thought the shots must have come from a Mannlicher-Carcano. "It was the first thing that came into my mind . . . across all the years . . . a Carcano."

⊕

1.
The
Town

Terni is seventy miles northeast of Rome. Situated about four hundred feet above sea level on the edge of the Apennines, the city lies on a flat and wide plain—the valley of the Nera River—surrounded by a circle of olive-colored hills. For all their haunting beauty, these hills were no bulwarks against attack in ancient times. Then, in the land now known as Italy, Terni, like Rome, was one of hundreds of diverse and self-contained communities. Most were vulnerable.

Terni had been no stranger to barbarism. Over the ages it had been invaded and sacked and so much destroyed that what remained of the past—such as baths built at the time of Christ, the Faustus Amphitheatre, dating from 32 A.D., a twelfth-century cathedral—were counterpoint to what the city became in the nineteenth century: a place of steel and guns.

As the poor man of the continent, long torn by internal strife and foreign influence, Italy had lived and died by many guns. Some were aimed at Italians; later, the same guns might be fired by Italians. But victims being greater in number than victories, the soldiers of Italy had more occasion to face than to capture the rifles of France, Austria, and Germany. They needed a rifle of their own.

By the mid-nineteenth century Italy had been invaded by sea, pillaged and overrun by land; there was, at that time, only one government on the Italian peninsula which could coalesce this divided people, provide military leadership, and ultimately bring nationhood to Italy. This was the government of Piedmont, the independent kingdom in the northwest. Piedmont existed, in part, because its dynasty, the House of Savoy, had a proven resourcefulness and longevity, and consequently the kingdom was regarded by the powers of Europe as a logical buffer zone between Austria and France. Turin, the capital of Piedmont, was also the capital of Italian engineering.

It was at the arms factory in Turin that the basic rifle of the Italians was designed and developed, principally by Lieutenant Colonel Salvatore Carcano. An obscure and unassuming man, who had been born in Varese (Lombardy) in 1827, Carcano emigrated to

Piedmont in 1849, where he was immediately employed at the arms factory of Turin. There, his mechanical skills were quickly recognized, and he was rapidly promoted because of his inventiveness and organizational capabilities.

The only thing that equaled Carcano's love of weapons was his love of family. The father of twelve boys, he had a full life, divided as it was between sons and guns. His character and disposition won him friends; his results won him the respect and admiration of his fellow artisans and of his superiors.

Carcano would never be as publicized as Colt, as commercially successful as Browning, as prolific with designs as Maxim, or as methodical as Mauser in his pursuit of one fundamental firearm. Yet, quietly, efficiently—in a land not then efficient—Carcano worked on his rifle, inventing, redesigning, improving, incorporating the refinements and advances of others.

In 1871, ten years after Italy had become a nation, King Victor Emmanuel, of the House of Savoy, moved the capital from Florence to Rome. The unification of Italy was complete. Metternich had once said, "Italy is just a geographic expression." No longer was this so. Freed to chart a very uncertain future after more than fifteen centuries of fragmentation and foreign domination, the new political entity had need for land reform, an educational system, productive agriculture, industrial and technical skills, a strengthened economy. Troops with weapons would help insure the future.

The king dispatched an officer to Terni.

⊕

SPEECH GIVEN BY HIS EXCELLENCY, THE GENERAL RICOTTI, SECRETARY OF WAR, ON THE OCCASION OF THE LAYING OF THE FIRST BRICK OF THE ARMS WORKS OF TERNI, MAY 2, 1875

Gentlemen: I express my most sincere wishes that this day will open a new era of richness and prosperity for the Terni Valley. Not long from now, a grandiose factory of the State will rise here, and it will give jobs and honest salaries to a considerable number of workers and, therefore, be an advantage to the city. Supplied with the best machinery it will, I hope, be able to compete with the most renowned arms factories abroad both for the quality and for the quantity of its products.

Terni already possesses various factories rightly renowned in private industry, but its present industrial level is nothing but the embryo of what the city can and must be; and truly, how can we imagine a more lucky combination of natural resources for mechanical constructions than we have here in Terni? From the Nera and the Velino an incredible amount of dynamic energy, free and everlasting, is produced. There are inexpensive construction materials in abundance, there is a fertile landscape, the climate is good, the geographic position is most fortunate, there is a calm population with an intelligent and industrious tradition; Terni has, in other words, all the prerequisites to achieve the highest level of industrial production.

In completing on this site this most important military factory, the government has certainly taken into consideration the interests of the State. But in its decision a great role was played by the belief that this will be a good start for the exploitation of the natural industrial richness of the countryside. And I am sure that Terni will fully respond to this trust for the good and the fame of Italy and of itself.

With this belief, in the name of His Majesty, the King of Italy, Vittorio Emanuele II, I lay the first brick of the Arms Factory of Terni.

When the wind was right, one might get the scent of growing things from the slopes of Terni's nearby hills. Sometimes a foundry worker and his family would hike the five miles to where the Velino River plunges 650 feet in a series of cataracts. Here, in this particularly beautiful corner of Umbria, the view was

both gentle and wild—opening either at one's feet down the olive hills toward the verdant valley or, with a slight turn and an upward look, into the mists and crashing waters called the Cascata delle Marmore. There, with the spray to cool the air of hot summer days, the family might picnic and drink wine and enjoy life before the week's work began.

The waterfalls were, perhaps, Terni's first manifestation of industry and inventiveness, a most impressive hydraulic creation of the third century before Christ. The Roman consul Manius Curius Dentatus had carved an artificial channel to enable otherwise stagnant lake waters to fall, with the Velino, into the river Nera. For two thousand years the Cascata delle

Marmore had conditioned the valley and its vegetation. The Velino into the Nera, the Nera through Terni to Narni and then to Orte and confluence with the Tiber, which would flow through Rome until it relieved itself of its waters and its wastes in the Tyrrhenian Sea and the ceaseless currents of the Mediterranean.

There was a steel mill, the Società di Terni, and in the mountains an easily available and abundant supply of lignite, a brownish-black coal to stoke the fires and make metal turn red hot, then white and malleable. In 1875, when General Ricotti laid the first brick at Terni, there existed the ten-year-old Martin process, of French origin, the precursor of the basic open-hearth furnace. By this, pig and scrap could be made into steel by first melting a good grade of pig iron, then adding selected wrought-iron scrap, which, under the influence of preheated air that increased the flame temperature, produced alloys whose carbon content could be regulated. This was important, for it had been found that mild steels with carbon content, strength, and ductility midway between carbon-free wrought iron, on the one hand, and high-carbon crucible steel, on the other, were most useful for the greatest variety of machinery and engineering. The mild steels were difficult to produce without the correct melting temperatures. The regenerative brick checkerwork employed in the Martin process, for preheating air, provided the answer.

The arms factory at Terni, the Royal Arms Works, had been designed by British engineers and furnished with Greenwood machinery of British design and manufacture, and in its first year of operation was able to yield one hundred rifles a day for the new Italy. As Italian engineering developed, the English machinery was replaced with equipment of native design and construction.

Though it would undergo further modifications over the years, the Carcano bolt-action rifle was adopted in 1891 as Italy's official military shoulder weapon. Salvatore Carcano, by this time arms controller of the Turin Arsenal, had incorporated in this model a clip and magazine which at once converted his single-shot rifle into a six-shot repeater. It was an Austrian, Ferdinand Ritter von Mannlicher, who had made this fundamental contribution to the rifle, which is now formally known as the Mannlicher-Carcano, less formally as *Il novantuno* ("the ninety-one"). Mannlicher was a genius in his field, producing not just mere designs, but actual weapons that anticipated bolt actions and magazine and semiautomatic features later used in the rifles of France, Germany, Belgium, Switzerland, Holland, England, Greece, and even in the basic infantry arm of the United States throughout the Second World War and beyond—the Garand.

The 91, named for the year of its first manufacture, was the principal weapon of the Italian army which, in World War I, fought alongside the Allies; it would continue as the principal weapon of the Italian army which, in World War II, fought against the Allies. It gained experience between the wars. It was extensively and effectively employed during the campaign in Ethiopia, in late 1935 and early 1936, when 250,000 Italian troops, most of them equipped with 91s, conquered that African nation. The 91 saw further dress rehearsal during the Spanish Civil War, 1936–1939: here was an opportunity for Italy to test weapons and tactics and troops under different combat conditions. Ultimately there were at least 100,000 Italian soldiers, armed with 91s, fighting for Franco against the Spanish Republic.

$\oplus$

In the late 1930s, when Terni's population numbered thirty-seven thousand, a change took place. Italy had gone to war with Ethiopia and the army needed more guns; the navy required more armor plate and projectiles. And so, in sight of the ruins of Terni's ancient baths and Temple of the Sun, new construction began. The iron-and-steel mill was expanded, the Royal Arms Works was given increased capacity. To meet these greater needs the engineers looked once more to the Velino's cataracts for the hydroelectric power that, beginning in the late nineteenth century and continuing into the twentieth, had already influenced the siting of industry and the gradual transformation of the city from a modest agricultural center to the largest industrial complex in central Italy.

When Mussolini made the trains run on schedule, the trip from Rome to Terni took under two hours. The Via Flaminia, an ancient and important Roman artery, had been little improved, and aside from army lorries making the dusty journey, most traffic came to and departed from Terni by rail. But by 1940 the road to Terni had been widened and repaved to accommodate the increased traffic to and from Rome. Now, generals, ministers of state, industrialists, couriers went back and forth with great frequency, and around the clock, trucks and rail cars were loaded with armor plate, projectiles, and guns.

On June 10, 1940, although the Nazis were already within thirty-five miles of Paris and the French surrender was but twelve days away, Benito Mussolini declared war on Great Britain and France. "We are the foxes, the Germans the bisons," one report had him saying. "They break through and we enter."

Elsewhere, Russia had defeated Finland, some of whose troops were equipped with Mannlicher-Carcanos purchased years before from Italy. Belgium had abruptly capitulated to Hitler; the 335,000 English and French troops trapped along the North Sea beaches at Dunkirk had been evacuated; and the Battle of Britain had begun.

America remained confused and indecisive; notwithstanding the fact that the German blitzkrieg had signaled the arrival in modern warfare of heavily armored tanks, the United States sold Mussolini almost 250,000 tons of scrap iron and steel. Japan, still preparing for war and relying heavily upon generous stockpiles of American scrap, acquired another 1 million tons, driving the price per ton down by the magnitude of her orders and the eagerness of Americans to unload.

In Washington, the Defense Advisory Board began to wonder whether, with scrap yet to be listed as an embargoed strategic material, the President's signature on a bill to create a two-ocean navy would be backed by the steel required, or only by the ink.

To help England keep her supply lines open, President Roosevelt traded fifty overage destroyers to the British fleet in return for the right to lease naval and air bases ranging, geographically, from Newfoundland to Antigua.

The United States, still a nation technically at peace, enacted conscription, and 17 million men, from twenty-one to thirty-five, registered for the draft, although the domestic-weapons shortage was so acute inductees initiated their military service with broomsticks as rifles.

President Roosevelt was elected to an unprecedented third term. While calling for fifty thousand military aircraft a year, he reviewed the ninety-four thousand enlisted men and officers of the First Army. Nowhere in sight was there an automatic weapon.

That was a part of the year 1940.

⊕

That same year, at the Royal Arms Works, in Terni, seven thousand men, divided into three round-the-clock shifts, produced twenty-five hundred 91s every twenty-four hours. Although coming from identical outpourings of a mass-production process, each weapon was stamped with its own numbers and markings; together, these markings would brand each gun as a unique entity. One such entity was identified thus:

—"CAL. 6.5" gave the bore, the inside diameter of the barrel, expressed in millimeters;
—"RE TERNI" indicated the place of manufacture, "RE" signifying *Regio Esercito* ("Royal Army");
—The crown, as a proof mark, and "TNI," together attested to an inspection of the barrel by an official of the Royal Arms Works, in Terni;
—"P.G.," the initials of the designer who furnished the bolt handle;
—"S.D.," the initials of the inspector of the rifle;

—"ROCCA," for Giuseppe Rocca, owner of a machine shop in a northern province, and manufacturer and supplier of the bolt cocking piece;

—a serial number and letter, in combination, were stamped into the metal, giving a particular unit identity; no other gun would be so marked. One was branded, forever, "C2766."

And, finally, the year of manufacture was impressed. For C2766 it was "1940." C2766 was indeed identifiable, with all of the above marks, meanings, signs, and signatures. Clearly, born in Terni, in 1940.

Although there was a trend to equip a certain percentage of her riflemen with semiautomatic weapons when she was about to enter the war, Italy looked first to a 1938 modification of the old 91. The 91/38, or, more simply, Model 38, was made to accommodate a new cartridge of larger caliber—the 7.5-millimeter Carcano. But with war imminent, a complete conversion to the new caliber was quite impossible. Even though Italy could produce sufficient ammunition, she could not quickly enough replace the 6.5-millimeter 91s with the 7.5-millimeter Model 38s for which that ammunition would be made. If she recalled from the field the 91s in use, for conversion to the new and larger caliber, thereby giving those weapons greater firepower and a muzzle velocity of almost half a mile per second, then her troops would find themselves temporarily without combat strength. There was no way for Italy to produce enough Model 38s to substitute new rifles for old, at the front, while still maintaining an adequate supply of 38s for the expanding war effort. Therefore, the 6.5-millimeter cartridge was re-established for the new 91/38 weapons, and the 38s already produced were rebarreled.

Even as the 38s were modified, other slight changes were brought to the original 91. The barrel was shortened to provide greater ease of handling; the sight-graduation system was altered to provide for sighting in on closer targets. The detachable knife-bayonet was kept (earlier models had had, at first, a permanently fixed knife-bayonet, then a folding bayonet permanently attached). This latest model was called the 41, for the new year.

In the lineage of the 91 there was even an Italian youth carbine. Urged on by an insatiable capacity for mimicry, Mussolini, aware that Hitler was rewarding mothers who produced boys and, when they were five or six, rewarding the boys with exposure to weapons, while obtaining their promise to become soldiers for a reawakened and rearming Germany, desired to commence training Italian boys for war. A scaled-down 91 carbine, complete with folding bayonet, was produced. Except for size, it was a replica of its larger brother. In the 1930s, about thirty thousand youth carbines were manufactured at the Fabbrica Nazionale d'Armi, in Brescia. Officially made for the Italian Fascist Youth party, the somewhat miniaturized rifle used only blank ammunition and the tip of its bayonet was dulled. Its full name was the Moschetto Regolomentare Ballila Modelo 1891 Ridotto, meaning "Ballila Regulation Musket Model 1891, Reduced." The American GI, in the mid-1940s, would covet these small rifles and bring them back to the States as among the rarest of military prizes.

⊕

From 1891 to the end of Italy's military production in World War II, millions of Mannlicher-Carcano rifles were manufactured. However, Model 91 was of such solid and successful design that it remained unchanged in its essentials over these more than five decades and was used until 1945, when the Italian army was armed with Lee-Enfield rifles.

Model 91—and, thus, C2766—is a multiloading weapon provided with a fixed and central magazine containing six cartridges. The bolt is of a rotating and sliding type. The barrel is a steel tube with a slightly truncated cone shape, internally rifled. The rifling consists of four helical, right-hand, variable twist grooves, increasing the rate of turn of the escaping bullet from one revolution in nineteen inches at the breech to one revolution in eight inches at the muzzle. It is this turning of the bullet which helps it find its mark. A bullet is pristine immediately on exiting from a rifle muzzle, when it moves in a straight line with a spinning motion and maintains a uniform trajectory with but a minimum of nose surface striking the air through which it passes. When the straight line of flight of a bullet is altered as it strikes an object, it starts to wobble or become irregular in flight, a condition called "yaw." A bullet with yaw has a greater surface exposed to material it strikes, since the target is struck not only by the nose of the bullet—its smallest striking surface—but also by the bullet's sides. This is why a wound of exit is frequently much greater than the wound of entry. If a man is hit in the head with a 6.5-millimeter bullet shot from a Mannlicher-Carcano at a distance of about one hundred yards, the bones of the skull are sufficient to deform and deflect the bullet, causing it to expend energy adequate to blow out the other side of the head. The spinning of the bullet is often compared with the spiral motion of the forward pass thrown by a football player.

Externally, the barrel is provided with a metal band to which the front sight is fixed. At about three-fourths of the way along the barrel's length, there is a second band to which the rear sight is attached, a V notch graduated from 500 to 1500 meters on some models, from 300 to 1000 meters on others, or just a plain fixed notch, rigid and unadjustable, on still other models. The barrel is screwed to the receiver, a cylindrical box with longitudinal grooves through which the bolt slides, and with a vertical opening for the passage of the clip and the magazine spring.

The loading and firing mechanism of Model 91 consists of the bolt, receiver, ejector and trigger device, and magazine. The shaped stock is made of wood.

Ancillaries include the bayonet stud, the iron butt plate for protecting the stock, the hand grip for avoiding burns when gripping the hot weapon, the sling, and the cleaning rod.

Model 91 has many parts, but is well made and well assembled into a sturdy weapon considered very effective, especially when used at relatively short ranges—not over 300 meters. The maximum range is 2800 meters, about 3100 yards, or roughly three football-field lengths shy of two miles. It is considered very solid, very serviceable, well designed for rugged military action, trouble free, and, in the hands of a good marksman, very accurate. In fact, its caliber and accuracy have caused some to regard the Carcano as *umanitario*—humanitarian. Unlike so many automatic weapons of larger caliber, the 91s, including C2766, fire a bullet of modest size, and each shot could be aimed.

A lieutenant in the Argyll and Sutherland Highlanders described an experience that happened late in 1942, toward the end of the British Eighth Army's campaign against Italian and German forces in North Africa.

"Strangely enough, it all happened so quickly. There was this long line of the enemy coming in to surrender. I remember thinking how dirty and unkempt they were, and how ill-fitting their uniforms. Odd, how one thinks of things like that at such a time.

"To my left and behind me some of the NCOs were rounding up prisoners and getting them into some sort of formation. I waved my pistol at the men in front with their hands up as a sign to them to join the others.

"Suddenly, one young German—couldn't have been much more than sixteen—decided to run for it. He must have been crazy, you know, to think he could escape, and if he could, that he would survive in the desert—although, I must say, there might have been food and water in many of the abandoned tanks out there.

"I shouted for the boy to stop, but, although I knew the word in German, *Halt*, didn't think to use it. One of the NCOs dashed over to a pile of Italian Carcanos, just given up. He had only his pistol. He picked up a rifle—I didn't imagine it was still loaded, but then, we were not all that careful all of the time.

"The German must have been a bloody seventy-five meters or so down the road when the NCO dropped to his knee, took aim, and fired. The boy fell. We went out there and picked him up. The bullet had passed through his back and out his shoulder. If it had been an automatic weapon the best the boy could have had would be a large entry hole and a jagged, horrible tear on the exit side. Dashed brutal size some of those automatics—knock out a tank if you please.

"The boy was still alive. We brought him to a field hospital and they patched him up. Ten days or so later I saw him, on a stretcher, but propped up, don't you know, being transferred to another place for prisoners. He obviously was getting better. You could see it by the smiles he gave to other German prisoners, and by the gestures of his arms. Almost like a parson after Sunday service."

The lieutenant hesitated a moment, then continued. "I took a look at that rifle. I was amazed it had brought the boy down. After all, the weapon was new to the NCO, but it clearly was simple enough to operate and damned accurate. It did its job, all right. Let him hit that boy where he wanted, just enough to do him partially in. Good shot, that NCO. The Carcano, too. Not brand new, but new enough. It was stamped 'Made in nineteen-forty.' Seen some action, too, from the looks of it. Good show, it was. You see, it's not every rifle permits you—even if you're good—to aim in quickly and carefully, to provide an *intelligent* wound."

The Allies struck in Sicily two months after the

Axis had surrendered in North Africa. "Operation Husky" was the name for the combined amphibious operation across the Mediterranean, the first such attack on Europe. Through the lacy fringe of water surrounding the island, landing craft came in, disgorging 160,000 men and ton after ton of supplies.

The ten Italian divisions on Sicily offered little resistance. They had, by this time, virtually given up on Fascism and fighting. Two weeks after the invasion began, Mussolini was overthrown by the Fascist Grand Council, in its first meeting in more than twenty years. A provisional government was formed under Marshal Pietro Badoglio, and immediately the Allies were contacted regarding a possible armistice.

Thirty-nine days after the landings, even though the three Nazi divisions had been able to fight with ferocity across the island and from their vantage points on the rocky slopes of the eleven-thousand-foot Mount Etna, Sicily was conquered. Italy had effectively been eliminated from the war, and the invasion of the Italian peninsula was at hand.

In the Sicilian campaign tens of thousands of Carcanos were abandoned by Italian soldiers giving up on war. Some of these rifles had been made in Terni, in different years, including the year 1940. Some of these quickly became the possessions of partisans in Sicily and were used by them against Germans during the thirty-nine days of the Allied campaign. Some, in covert and clandestine ways, were brought into Italy by young men, returning to their land, anxious to participate with the Allies in the final fight against the occupying Germans. From this point forward, the 91 was the right hand of the partisans.

$\oplus$

Field Marshal Kesselring complained of the partisans, of their bands "mostly composed of escaped prisoners of war who made their appearance in the rear of the Tenth Army, as a rule trying to fight their way across the front. . . ."

On March 23, 1944, a few months before the fall of Rome, some partisans planted a bomb at a point on the Via Rasella, where each day, at the same hour, a detachment of German police troops marched through the heart of the city. Exploding on schedule, the bomb killed thirty-two men.

Kesselring argued with Hitler and Himmler that to deport every able-bodied male in Rome to the labor camps of Germany, in reprisal, would be to limit and even paralyze railroads and supply lines in Italy. He argued for permission "to achieve a deterrent effect . . . an honest effort to exercise humanity." Consequently, he issued and signed an order specifying that for every one of the thirty-two Germans who died, ten Romans should be executed. The field marshal felt that this, rather than deportation, was more in compliance with international law.

Not finding the required quota in the "Via Tasso" (the prison the Gestapo had made out of a sealed five-story apartment building, which, thereafter, was known to the Italians by the name of the street on which it was located), Kesselring's officers rounded up any Roman suspected of harboring anti-Fascist thoughts. Because their zeal was great, they were not careful in their counting. Instead of rounding up just 320 men, they found themselves with 335. The prisoners were marched into one of the Fosse Ardeatine caves, where all were killed by machine-gun fire. The bodies were covered with lime. A dynamite blast sealed the entrance to the death chamber.

Kesselring said he had loved the Italians. Now he was angry and hated them. "The partisan war," he wrote, "was a complete violation of international law and contradicted every principle of clean soldierly fighting."

In Naples, after the German retreat, twenty hastily made coffins were carried into a schoolhouse and surrounded by flowers. There was a strange odor, flowers and the sweet, sickly smell of death. There were mourners for the young partisans, who had been laid out with great grief and great haste.

There weren't flowers enough to cover or hide the dirty feet—little feet—protruding from several of the coffins. For these were coffins made for children, and some of the children, just old enough to fight the Germans, were too tall, in the end.

For fourteen days, as a band of partisans, the twenty children, armed with Carcanos and bullets stolen from the Germans, had fought. Then, just before the Allies swept past Naples, the children were cornered and killed.

Outside the entrance to the schoolhouse, two adult partisans talked. They had viewed the coffins. One, Raffaele Bertoldo, held a Carcano taken hours before from the hand of a child. He looked at its markings and, seeing something familiar, calmly remarked to the other, "My brother lived in Terni." He shook his head, nodding sadly toward the schoolhouse over his shoulder. His face was taut with bitterness as he calmly, coldly stated: "For the children it is finished. Not for this rifle." Again his eyes searched the gun's markings. "Nineteen-forty. A child, too."

⊕

The 91/38 and 91/41 models were in continual production until the Allied-Italian armistice in 1943, and even afterward. From Sicily to the Po Valley, the Italian boot had not been an easy fit. There had been nine months of fighting northward from the toe before the U.S. Fifth Army marched into Rome. On a June evening in 1944, the Americans entered the Piazza Venezia. The people were grateful. The Germans were gone. The Eternal City had not been leveled. This summer night the only bombardment was the explosion of emotion—the cheering, the flowers tossed at soldiers atop tanks, the fruit handed GIs, the kisses freely given, the Chianti poured in profusion.

But it would be another eleven months after this night on which Rome became an "open" city until the unconditional-surrender agreement of German headquarters in Italy. In those eleven months, fighting and killing continued, and Italian partisans, in combat alone or joined with American forces against the Germans, accounted for many enemy casualties.

There was an incident in September 1944 in the southern part of Tuscany. An American infantry company had captured five German soldiers and several officers riding in two American jeeps. The retreating Germans had obviously taken the jeeps from Americans, and the GIs and their commanding officer were trying to find out how they had done this, and whether they had killed any Americans.

It was hot that September, and the valley was arid. The Germans—under direction of an American captain—had divested themselves of their rifles, automatic weapons, pistols, packages of ammunition, and other supplies. All these, stacked on the hard-packed bare ground between the jeeps, made a heap of black in the white dust of the overlong, obstinate summer.

Several partisans came upon this scene. "They approached, slowly," related the captain. "One poked about in the pile of weapons and paraphernalia. He reached down and withdrew a weapon, a rifle. He turned to me. 'Captain, it is mine,' he said, and pointing at the Germans, he continued, 'These are the ones who killed your brothers in our village, raped our women, stole supplies. There is no doubt. Look'— he held out the rifle—'it is mine . . . a Carcano.' He walked closer to me. 'Captain, here'—he pointed at some markings on the gun—'Terni, nineteen-forty, as my own.'

"I could see it was a Carcano all right, but of course other rifles had been made in that same arms works that same year. Still, it was a coincidence, the Carcano, the American jeeps. And it was too damn warm to argue about things like that.

"I waved to my men. We climbed into our half-track and drove off a hundred, maybe hundred fifty, yards. We stopped. Even the idling of the engine did not obscure the sharp crack of rifle fire, a good number of shots, seconds later, from around the bend where we'd just been.

"You know, it's a picture I didn't see happen, but I can see it as though I was there. The German uniforms were dark. Now there was another heap of black, probably right next to the pile of stuff lying on that miserable dried-out ground.

"I heard one of my men mumble something about 'too hot to be taking in prisoners.' And another asked one of those stupid after-the-fact questions: 'Think it was his gun? . . . He sure acted like it was a long lost friend.'

"Hell, as I think back on it, between fighting and trying to feed themselves, the partisans didn't have time for prisoners, either. I looked back as our half-track moved out and picked up speed. There was nothing I could see. I guess I'm glad. We were all so cool about slaughter, now that I think about it, back there in that goddamned heat."

$$\oplus$$

During the years of fighting in Italy, even as the Germans fell back, they continued to force production out of Italy's faltering war machine. Virtually up until the day Rome fell, the Royal Arms Works, in Terni, made 91s. In April 1944 ten thousand of these rifles were manufactured for Germany, with Germans in command of the factory. These would be the last, for, like Rome, Terni would soon be liberated. A message signed simply, "Roosevelt, Churchill," was dropped by Allied aircraft over Rome and other major Italian cities. The message was urgent:

The time has come for you, the Italian people, to consult your own self-respect and your own interests and your own desire for a restoration of national dignity, security and peace. The time has come for you to decide whether Italians shall die for Mussolini and Hitler—or live for Italy, and for civilization.

Throughout the war years, despite a constantly increasing aerial attack, only one bomb fell on the Royal Arms Works in Terni. This occurred on August

11, 1943. There was slight damage to one unimportant structure, but this was no impediment to production. There was a dog fight that day between Allied and German planes. Perhaps some bombardier, making his run, was distracted or his aim thrown off target by a violent movement of his aircraft. Nobody was hurt at the arms works, but the director and fifteen others who had fled to the safety of a nonmilitary target, a wool factory across the street, were killed when that factory was bombed into oblivion.

$$\oplus$$

Years later, after the war, after the splitting of the atom, and after the landing on the moon, there was a man, heavy-set and jovial, who would reflect upon it all. Francesco Crescentini had never seen a nuclear detonation or the firing of a giant rocket leaving its pad for space. But he was no stranger to the destruction and devastation and the fire and fury of war.

Terni was his home. There he had lived through the political turmoil and the despair of the twenties. There he had worked in the Royal Arms Works, starting as a young man, not long after Italy's attack on Ethiopia. Later he supervised the production of more tens of thousands of 91s than he could ever count. There, during World War II, he had lived through more than one hundred aerial bombardments of his city, during which 80 per cent of Terni was destroyed and eight thousand of its citizens were killed—and buried, mostly, in mass graves. There, in Terni, he had remained after the armistice in 1943, and there had been forced to produce still more 91s for the retreating German forces.

There, after the war ended in 1945, he stayed. By the tens of thousands now the 91s came back like salmon to their spawning grounds. In Italy, as generally in Europe, gun ownership is restricted and regulated. Peacetime restored some semblance of order. Partisans turned in their weapons. Some were worn with use, some with abuse. Some were intact, some scarred. Some, like torsos without limbs, were missing extremities. They came in without bolts, without sights, without slings.

Some had been used to kill, and some had not. Some had been to North Africa and some to the Balkans. Some had known desert heat, some the breeze sweeping across Sicily from the blue Mediterranean. Some had known the mud near Cassino, the beachhead at Anzio, the snows of the Alps and the Apennines.

And the Royal Arms Works, that great, long, low bastionlike building with its huge inner courtyard that would have confused the untutored into thinking it the villa of a very rich and powerful man—this great building became a warehouse. Never again would new weapons be produced there. Instead, rifles would be repaired and barrels manufactured or rebored for the Caribinieri, the police force of Italy that is part of the army.

Crescentini was still active, full of restless energy. Occasionally he would go to Rome; more usually, he would turn his car toward the mountains. Taking the Valnerina State Highway, he would follow the winding road past the Cascata delle Marmore, a sterile sight. The waters flowed into and through a hydroelectric plant supplying energy to Terni's rebuilt industry, industry whose smokestacks disgorged pollution that fouled the plain and blackened the roof tiles of houses high in the hills. For the public, the Cascata would flow only on holidays, Saturday nights, and Sundays. On these occasions the waters—being unnecessary to the power plant that converted their force into electricity during the work week—would be permitted to flow, to cascade, to create mists. On Saturday nights the falls would be illuminated in order that those who wanted to contemplate unnatural things might have light to see.

On he would drive, on to Rieti, and there visit, as he had so many times, the Franciscan sanctuary clinging to the rocky walls of a hill, built around the hermitage where Saint Francis of Assisi went to live with some of his disciples in about 1217 A.D. Crescentini would talk with the Padre, by now an old friend; he would light a candle, he would leave a coin. He would curse the stairs he had climbed because they were steep and almost as tiring to descend. He would curse the winding road leading back to Terni. Sometimes he would be at the steel-mill gate when the 6:00 a.m. shift began its afternoon exodus. He would see the men on bicycles and motor scooters, tired by their labors, moving surely and slowly toward their houses, hardly noticing each other or the intermittent cars.

He would come to the building where he had worked so many, many years—during the forties, fifties, sixties. The lowering afternoon sun would give exceptional warmth to its yellowish-orange stucco walls. He would think—it was always the same thought—how the Royal Arms Works had lived with four masters: the king; Mussolini; General Badoglio, the head of the provisional government following the armistice in 1943; the new Republic, proclaimed after a referendum in 1946.

"Four lovers," he would think. Then, more from compassion than disrespect, as with the Italians who in a card game or during a soccer match curse God and Christ and the Virgin but attend Mass on Sunday, he would nod his head toward the structure, now almost one hundred years old, and say aloud for the world, his own small world to hear, *"Vecchia puttana!"*—"old whore!"

⊕

2.
The
Trade

In the early 1950s Adam Hat Stores, Incorporated, was losing about $1 million annually. For a long time, beginning with its incorporation in New York State in 1924, its business had prospered, and at its height, the corporation owned some hundred retail stores throughout the United States. A good deal of its success was attributable to early sponsorship of prizefight broadcasts from Madison Square Garden. Millions of men listened to the radio; the hatted head became quite as much a symbol of virility as the gloved hand.

Several factors, however, caused a severe reversal for Adam Hat Stores. First, there was the advent of television. In comparison with radio, TV sponsorship was expensive and, in the case of the fights, beyond the reach of Adam. Gillette (razor blades) outbid Adam for the TV rights; Adam was not able to find another outlet for its advertising dollar, an outlet that would even begin to approach the value of its previous radio patronage of so many fights over so many, many years. In short order sales began to slip.

Second, there was the matter of wages and salaries for employees and managers in the stores. These had increased, and although they were absorbed by rising sales during the golden years of radio sponsorship, as a cost—an appreciable one—they began to create a pressure after the fights had shifted to Gillette.

Third, there was the increasing hatlessness of the American male. Men's tastes in clothes were becoming more informal. The *Proceedings of the Seventh Convention of the United Hatters, Cap and Millinery Workers International Union, May 1–6, 1950*, had this to say: "Since 1939 the number of fur felt hats produced in our industry has decreased approximately 28 per cent . . . this decline from 1947 on has been at the rate of approximately 10 per cent a year." The *Proceedings of the Eighth Convention, June 8–12, 1953*, reported "signs of recuperation and improvement" attributable, in part, to "an abnormal factor, such as the stimulus given to hat sales when President Eisenhower donned a Homburg for his inauguration." But the upsurge was ephemeral, and the *Proceedings of the Tenth Convention*, in 1959, said with a note of finality, "It can be seen from both production and employment decline that the men's hat and body industry has returned to its old long-term trend downwards."

And so, Adam Hat Stores, losing as much as $1 million a year in the early 1950s, was sold in 1954 to a company experienced and successful in the retail tire business. In 1956 the corporate name was changed to Adam Consolidated. The hundred-odd hat stores, still a losing proposition, were sold, chiefly to their managers, with payments spread over a number of years. It was the sale of the stores that provided Adam Consolidated with additional working capital not only to expand its tire business, whose outlets included Macy's, but for other venture situations. The tire business was expanded, and while consideration was given to building up the burgeoning conglomerate that already included a dozen or more subsidiary operations, a name change to Vanderbilt Tire & Rubber Company was contemplated. Dropping the Adam identification would have been prescient. President Eisenhower wore hats, but the next President would not. He never wore a hat.

It is doubtful that Alberto Bagnasco, an Italian attorney, knew Daniel Burnham's maxim: "Make no little plans; they have no magic to stir men's blood."

Bagnasco was in his late thirties, ambitious and well connected. In the mid-1950s he was secretary and assistant to the regional president of Sicily, and later was employed by the Roman newspaper *Il Tempo*. He had represented various commercial interests, including oil firms in Sicily. In his travels, he learned of plans by the Italian Ministry of Defense to liquidate its inventory of 91s in 1958. Bids would be sought on approximately 570,000 weapons, both serviceable and unserviceable. That inventory was no *little* plan. It had the magic to stir much blood.

Bagnasco contacted an attorney in Philadelphia—Andrew Farnese—with whom he had had other business dealings, regarding the possibility of interesting an American company in the hundreds of thousands of Carcanos about to be sold. Yes, Farnese knew of a prospect, the H and D Folsom Arms Company, 154 Ludlow Street, Yonkers, New York.

In April 1875, just a month before General Ricotti laid the first brick of the Royal Arms Works in Terni, the legislature of the state of New Jersey passed an Act Concerning Corporations. Under its provisions, another gun industry was soon born, several thousand miles from Italy, when Henry and David Folsom incorporated the H and D Folsom Arms Company. The place of business was listed on the certificate of incorporation as the city of Jersey City. The company was formed for "the manufacturing, buying, selling, exporting, and importing of fire-arms, ammunition, and sporting goods. . . ." In 1892, a year after the 91 was adopted as Italy's standard shoulder arm, Folsom received authority to do business in the state of New York.

At its inception Folsom was a family business, and it remained one. But slightly more than half a century after its founding, the relatives and heirs were not in a position to continue the firm's activities. It was wartime, not the best of seasons for handling guns and ammunition unless one happened to be a large manufacturer. Millions of men were in military service, and for those who remained in civilian life overtime work in defense industries and gasoline rationing placed restraints upon leisure pursuits. The market for sporting goods was hurt. By the unanimous consent of its stockholders, Folsom filed a certificate of dissolution with the state of New Jersey. It was December 1942.

In August 1943 Folsom surrendered its authority to do business in the state of New York. The next month, September, Italy surrendered to the Allies.

But man is both carnivorous and convivial, wiping away the blood while toasting with the wine. Let not retribution inhibit restoration: it is the human, not the economic, side of man that suffers in war. Only people die. Nations and businesses come back. So it was with Italy. And so with Folsom Arms.

Two brothers, Louis and Irving Feldsott, took over the Folsom company after its dissolution, and in the postwar years built it up as a wholesaler in sporting goods, including various weapons. When Andrew Farnese called from Philadelphia with information concerning surplus Italian Carcanos, his message received attention. The Feldsotts saw the sales potential of the 91s, but lacked the necessary financial resources to capitalize upon the opportunity. A friend put them in touch with a possible sponsor, a company called Adam Consolidated.

⊕

Because of what had happened to the hat business, and because there was no sign it would recover to its former condition, Adam Consolidated necessarily altered its managerial perspective. Dealing in rifles, even indirectly, as financier, was nothing really different for Adam; guns were another product—that simple—and another opportunity for return on investment. Why consider the link between money and muzzle? Who did? Who does? In business, many say, it is the *bottom line* that counts. That alone.

So Adam Consolidated took a look at the business at hand and took a look at the business potentials in a firearms transaction, and felt somewhat better. Things looked positive, indeed. There clearly was a market for the Carcanos, and no examination of the entire matter, from purchase in Italy, to transportation, to sale in the United States disclosed any elements of risk.

Three American firms entered the competition for

the 91s that the Italian Defense Ministry was selling; Adam Consolidated, in conjunction with the Feldsott brothers, won the bidding with a total offer of $1,776,000 for the approximately 570,000 guns. In keeping with business practice on such a transaction, guarantees of one-third the amount, or $592,000, were given by the Banco di Roma. Irving Feldsott went to Italy to work out contractual details, where he received assistance from Alberto Bagnasco. The contract signed was between the Ministry of Defense and Adam Consolidated. The documents were agreed to in an atmosphere of warmth.

In Act I of Shaw's *Major Barbara*, the Salvation Army officer importunes her father, Europe's chief manufacturer and purveyor of weapons, to visit Army headquarters:

UNDERSHAFT: May I ask, have you ever saved a maker of cannons?

BARBARA: No. Will you let me try?

UNDERSHAFT: Well, I will make a bargain with you. If I go to see you tomorrow in your Salvation Shelter, will you come the day after to see me in my cannón works?

BARBARA: Take care. It may end in your giving up the cannons for the sake of the Salvation Army.

UNDERSHAFT: Are you sure it will not end in your giving up the Salvation Army for the sake of the cannons?

BARBARA: I will take my chance of that.

UNDERSHAFT: And I will take my chance of the other. Where is your Shelter?

BARBARA: In West Ham. At the sign of the cross. Ask anybody in Canning Town. Where are your works?

UNDERSHAFT: In Perivale St. Andrews. At the sign of the sword. Ask anybody in Europe.

The location of the Ministero della Difesa—the Italian Defense Department—is not quite so obvious. Even in Rome one must give the taxi driver the address, Via XX Settembre; the hotels and restaurants are better known. The building entrance suggests nothing warlike or militaristic, nor does one approach it through a clearing, as with the Pentagon, which dominates the landscape with its five-sided silhouette, its thousand-car parking lots, its active heliport.

At the Ministero della Difesa, one finds heavy, handsome wood doors; a wide-open, friendly, and roofed interior foyer with potted plants on the marble floors; a warm and courteous guard; a reception area dimly lit by flickering fluorescents bouncing off flaking paint; an atmosphere conducive—from the buyer's standpoint—to bidding: in more opulent surroundings he might be intimidated to raise his offer.

At the Ministero della Difesa in 1959, Feldsott and Bagnasco were satisfied: the price was right. They had the experience of others to assess. For example, the International Firearms Company of Montreal had over a period of time bought hundreds of thousands of Carcano rifles earlier surplused by the Italian government. Many of these were in such poor condition as a result of battlefield use or abandonment, subsequent improper storage, or previous stripping for parts that they were purchased not by the unit but by the pound. Upon arrival in Canada, defective elements were removed and salable rifles were constructed of components of three or more weapons. Some dealers even brought in rifles as "scrap"—a device often used to circumvent tariff regulations.

For Adam Consolidated, it was a clean, easy prospect: no war, and no piecemeal.

Specifically, of the debris and remnants of war, Adam Consolidated contracted for 6.5-millimeter Model 91/38s. In the contract there were about three of these deemed "efficient" for every two regarded as "inefficient." Some 5300 kilos (approximately 12,000 pounds) of parts were included in the contract price. Adam also purchased 2,608,704 rounds of ammunition, which were picked up and paid for as items separate from the surplus weapons, on three occasions:

August 8, 1960	652,176 cartridges 6.5 millimeter
July 21, 1961	1,304,352 cartridges 6.5 millimeter
June 6, 1962	652,176 cartridges 6.5 millimeter

The price was $13.57 per thousand, or somewhat more than a penny per bullet.

Adam Consolidated was to be the importer of the 91s and the financier of the transaction. However, as its business and holdings ran far afield from weapons, a new entity was created to act as distributor for rifles brought into the United States. Louis Feldsott was named president of this new corporation, Crescent Firearms, chartered under the laws of the state of New York, December 29, 1959. To protect its investment, Adam Consolidated installed its vice-president, Joseph Saik, as secretary-treasurer of Crescent Firearms.

Like many corporations, Crescent stated its proposed activities in the broadest possible language. Under its certificate of incorporation it might even purchase, lease, or otherwise acquire lands and buildings. But most germane to its initial or immediate aim was the second paragraph of the certificate:

The purposes for which it is to be formed are to do any and all of the things hereafter set forth to the same extent as natural persons might or could do in any part of the world, namely:—

To carry on the business of manufacturers and dealers in firearms, ordnance and munitions of every type and description, and for that purpose to manufacture, purchase, import, export, sell and generally deal in rifles, guns, pistols, cannons, bullets, cartridges, shells, casings, armor-piercing and other projectiles, torpedoes, missiles, mines, bombs, grenades, primers, detonators, fuses, wads, loading and reloading tools, ammunition hoisting, carrying and storing apparatus, shields, armor and protective coverings of all kinds, range-finding and sighting devices and other products of the same or a similar nature for military, naval, sporting, commercial or other uses.

In other words, the license of free enterprise.

Adam Consolidated . . . Crescent Firearms . . . Folsom Arms—all legitimate business entities, and their principals all honest and hard-working men. In time, because of C2766, they would be questioned about their interests and intentions. But the answers revealed, beyond any dispute, nothing other than a sincere interest in doing business, and a sincere intent to do well in business. The purveyor of guns is no different from the seller of automobiles. Both products are pleasurable to some and lethal to others, depending on use or abuse. The only difference is that the latter are watched and marked in their travels and trades, their users licensed according to standards—varying, perhaps, but standards nonetheless.

The men of Adam, Crescent, Folsom? As businessmen, no better or worse than others. As men, driven, as many are, to succeed. Interested in the good sale and the good life. This, of course, might be the epitaph of a whole civilization, not just that of a few individuals. With regrets, like prescience, minimal.

Man takes comfort in caste. The derelict does not usually disport himself on Main Street, or the banker on the Bowery. Accordingly, there are many buildings in New York City which have more than one address. In some cases this is a feature of physical planning and necessity; in some, a peculiarity of man's penchant for prestige. One enters the Waldorf

Astoria Hotel, if possible, from Park Avenue, not Lexington. One speaks of 30 Rockefeller Plaza, not of its Sixth Avenue address.

Not so with Crescent. Its office building at 2 West 37th Street had another entrance, at 404 Fifth Avenue. The former was Crescent's legal address; the latter was the address for Adam Consolidated. Around the corner from each other, yet purposeful in their proximity: Adam and Crescent had offices on the sixth floor, used the same receptionist, could be called at—and indeed were listed with—the same telephone number. If Bagnasco had been there the offices could have been A,B, and C. But he was not. Across the ocean, if not around the corner, he was, as in alphabetical order, a strategically placed middle-man.

3.
The
Traffic

Long before there would be a John F. Kennedy Center for the Performing Arts, with all its gleaming marble the gift of Italy, the propensity of the American people for firearms was attracting steel, if not stone, from abroad.

America—in the years of the great immigrations which ended early in the twentieth century—had held out her hands to the "teeming masses yearning to be free." After World War II she held out her hands once more. To the vanquished, as well as to her Allies who had suffered so much, there would be vast amounts of military and economic assistance.

Yet as the one hand gave, the other took—but more hardware than people, more rifles than refugees. Besides the memorabilia and spoils of war brought back to the States by returning servicemen —bayonets and guns and grenades and flags—there began to be an international traffic in firearms, with America a principal recipient. She had the cash, she had the markets. Millions of men had been taught to hunt men; surely, hundreds of thousands or millions would resume their prewar recreational pursuits of, or be newly converted to, target shooting and the hunting of animals as a sport. This would create a prodigious demand for weapons virtually unavailable to civilians during the war, as were automobiles, gasoline, and tires, when the need for America's industrial output was in theaters of combat.

In the years following World War II, the United States became the world's major dumping ground for obsolete military weapons. The word "obsolete" is used advisedly: the fact that an army had been destroyed by the war and itself had become obsolescent in a political sense did not mean its captured weapons were unworkable, or could not be made operable with modest investments in repairs, restoration, and new or rebuilt parts. But it was not only wartime weapons that entered the pool of international trade. In many instances European nations also sold off rifles of newer issue as they were replaced by better weapons. This occurred in immense volume when NATO standardized its arms.

The international firearms traffic was manifest in

four distinct categories of imports. First, there was the trade in high-cost foreign shotguns, rifles, and handguns manufactured abroad specifically for the conspicuous and cash-rich United States market for sporting firearms.

Second, there was the low-cost, newly made .22 caliber foreign nonmilitary handgun, heavily sold through the mails. Later to be called, and widely heralded as, the "Saturday night special" (for its use in crimes of passion after an evening of imbibing), this type of weapon featured heavily in the dismal statistics by which Americans measured their frontier spirit in a modern era.

Third, there developed a trade, small, but evident, in high-caliber military surplus such as bazookas, antitank guns, and mortars—without live ammunition. The market for these items was largely in suburbia, where some thought the residence was made more attractive or, perhaps, more defensible, through the sporting of artillery on the lawn. At the least, a cannon was good for conversation.

Fourth, there sprang up a rather considerable market for military-surplus arms, about 80 to 85 per cent center-fire rifles. These firearms opened up a large opportunity for profit-minded individuals or firms anxious to distribute low-cost sporting and target weapons at prices ranging from ten dollars to twenty-five dollars and up.

For this last category of weapons—weapons whose

numbers would grow into the millions—there were numerous justifications. Some said that if there were a problem, it was only one of cheapness and of availability to anonymous buyers through mail order. It was difficult, so the argument went, to legislate against cheapness, because of the unhappy precedent it would set. "Should we outlaw the sale of used cars under two hundred dollars to protect the teen-ager from this lethal instrument?"

Others suggested it was not senseless for Americans to have the opportunity to buy what they wanted with their own money, to serve their strictly private recreational purposes. In testimony before a Senate subcommittee, one arms dealer claimed: "The country-bred man who likes to hunt as his father did before him . . . discovers, because he knows guns, that this Mauser, made several decades ago to military specifications, has a finer action than any new American-made gun in the store. He sees that the price of thirty-five dollars compared to [that of] a new rifle saves him about one hundred dollars, which he sorely needs at home. So he buys the gun and discovers in the hunting field that it shoots straight and has safety qualities equal to or exceeding available bolt-action new-production sporting rifles."

A civil-rights, frontier-spirit, rugged-individualism synthesis sufficed on occasion. Again, the same enormously successful dealer argued before the subcommittee holding hearings on the gun trade: "I think there are many Americans concerned that hard-pressed federal officials may become so bent on protecting their wards from events which make up disturbing statistics that they overlook the task of protecting the sense of independence and self-reliance in our citizenry which cannot be measured by statistics. . . ."

Most frequently voiced of all the status quo supplications was the contention voiced in the same hearings that "Americans may like guns because they are reminiscent of the smell of the outdoors, military heroism, the intensity of the hunt, or merely because they are fascinated by the finely machined parts. Maybe the origin of a gun speaks of history; maybe the gun makes a man's home seem to him less vulnerable; maybe these feelings are more justified in the country than in the city; but, above all, many of us believe that these feelings are a man's own business. . . ."

And finally, as though to indicate that freedom and liberty were not reason enough for the uninhibited flow of firearms, some invoked the spirit of patriotism and world sanity. Testifying before the House Foreign Affairs Committee, a State Department official put it this way: "I am frank to say that when there are questions of surplus arms cropping up abroad, which another area is bidding for, it may very often be the better part of valor and indeed the best part of our foreign relations to have them imported into this country rather than float around."

In 1960—to take one year, as an example—315,000 surplus military rifles, valued at *under* five dollars each, entered the United States. Who could question such valor? Few would question such value! And soon, few would even keep such records: for budgetary reasons, it was argued, the Department of State had to reduce staff. Because of a turnover in department personnel, nobody knew who originated the order. But, suddenly, the Munitions Control Statistical Unit was made expendable. A representative of the State Department said in a later justification, that the unit was abolished "on the basis that it was the least harmful action in terms of all operations. We were apparently experiencing about a one hundred per cent increase in licensing workload without an increase in staff. To have reduced the number of personnel issuing licenses . . . would have been more detrimental than to abolish the Munitions Control Statistical Unit." And so it was: license, encourage the traffic in firearms, and only change the manner of measurement.

$\oplus$

Unlike automobiles, firearms do not suffer from built-in obsolescence. They are generally quite durable and can be expected to last almost indefinitely when given proper care. It is therefore not surprising that the market for secondhand firearms is almost as important as that for the new. Almost 50 per cent of rifles acquired in the United States are purchased used. The small number of firearms worn out through use is confirmed by manufacturers' advice that, in terms of rounds fired, the useful life of a gun ranges from ten thousand to one hundred thousand rounds, depending upon the quality and type of weapon, and the care it is given. No wonder that sales of foreign imports (most of them surplus military weapons), as well as sales of secondhand domestic rifles, accelerated in the postwar years. Much life remains in old guns, and this awareness was manifested by the figures for rifles alone:

Date	Surplus Rifles Imported
1948	4,104
1950	14,070
1952	26,970
1958	198,202
1960	315,000
1963	424,085
1965	729,392

To be an importer, one had only to register with the Office of Munitions Control, Department of State. To be a dealer—a person qualified to buy arms at wholesale and transport them through the mails—one had only to pay a one-dollar fee to the Treasury Department. With so modest a sum at stake, one enterprising entrepreneur advertised in a magazine reaching gun buffs: "For Sale—Guns, Buy Wholesale. Become a dealer, instructions, $1.00." The instruction provided was simply this: for another dollar, apply for a federal license. Many took advantage. No applicant was required to be fingerprinted or checked for a criminal record. It was estimated that one-half of the applicants were not bona fide dealers at all, but individuals who, by virtue of their dollar licenses, added significantly to the essentially unregulated interstate shipment of firearms by mail order. In California—a state with some of the most restrictive laws governing sales of firearms—existing laws were easily circumvented by unscrupulous dealers operating in a manner that respected neither business ethics nor public safety. Such dealers justified their sales of deadly weapons on the basis that a purchaser had to sign a certificate stating that he was not an ex-convict, a narcotics addict, or an alien. But such statements were totally worthless, as they did not have to be made under oath and were not verified. No further attempt was made to regulate the customer's opportunity to purchase a gun. On the contrary, it was all made easy. Seaport Traders, a California firm, counseled:

Dear Customer:
In order for us to send your pistol or revolver, you have to obtain a Federal Firearms License. Same can be obtained for $1.00 at your Federal Building or Post Office, same

place where Federal Liquor Licenses are issued. These licenses are issued at once without waiting and this will enable you to purchase any number of guns from us, not only just this one. Therefore, your time and money in obtaining this license will be well spent.

Sincerely yours,
SEAPORT TRADERS, INC.

Seaport Traders, one of the largest dealers in imported weapons, sold 11,427 surplus foreign revolvers and stub-barreled automatics by mail, from 1961 to 1963. Chicago's police-department records indicated that 4069 were purchased by residents of that city. Twenty-five per cent, or 948 of these, went to persons with criminal records.

⊕

Long before there was any federal firearms legislation, the Congress was helping to spread the guns around. Beginning in 1903 (the country was still so young that the "frontier" had officially been closed only eleven years earlier, and Arizona and New Mexico had not yet become states), a series of acts established a civilian marksmanship program. Its purposes were to promote small-arms practice, hold small-arms competitions, and loan or sell arms, ammunition, and targets necessary for the program.

By the early 1960s the director of civilian marksmanship (DCM), reporting to the secretary of the army, was helping support almost six thousand rifle and pistol clubs, with a total membership of about four hundred thousand. Colleges and schools whose curricula included marksmanship also qualified for benefits under a law directing that the secretary "shall provide for . . . the sale to members of the National Rifle Association (NRA) at cost . . . of the arms . . . and other supplies . . . for target practice."

Founded in 1871, the NRA had exerted a profound influence on America's singular position as the most violence-prone, gun-oriented nation on earth—a nation with virtually no firearms controls, a nation with more guns than all other countries combined.

The United States was not the only nation with a frontier in its history. Canada had hers. And Australia. The United States was not the only nation to have industrialized and urbanized in a very short period marked by social reordering: consider postwar Japan. But the United States was the only major nation where the presence of violence had been answered, in part, by pressure for greater "gunsmanship," as though arming more citizens—in a constantly accelerating spiral—were a civilizing influence. In other nations, the reverse was the case: the response to the presence of some armed groups within the society had not been to arm all men, but to restrict the use of weapons by all men.

The NRA liked to quote Article II of the Bill of Rights:

A well-regulated militia being necessary to the security of a free State, the right of the people to keep and bear arms, shall not be infringed.

The NRA headquarters building in Washington, D.C., carried these words on its façade—words reminiscent of George Bernard Shaw's comment that "the first prison I ever saw had inscribed on it, 'Cease to do evil, learn to do well,' but, as the inscription was on the outside, the prisoners could not read it."

Inside the NRA offices, behind the lobby display of rifles and revolvers, there was security and isolation from a fast-changing, 80-per-cent-urbanized society. But at the NRA it was still the era of the horse and buggy, and the militia; the existence of the automobile, a Department of Defense, and the "military-industrial complex" didn't make any difference. At the NRA, it was still Colonial times and the Wild West and the original Wounded Knee . . . and every man for himself.

Some, favoring what might be called the "Hemingway syndrome," suggested that America's gun culture existed because guns were symbols of masculinity. But then why have not men of other nations found guns to be essential to their confidence in manhood?

Some, clinging to the frontier as an explanation of America's gun culture, suggested that conquering the land and the American Indian was so much a part of our heritage it would take generations to forget we were no longer winning the West. But the superintendent of the census had officially closed the frontier in 1892, few living Americans have had any contact with the direct influence of the frontier, and for decades most Americans have lived in urban areas.

Some said that the American gun culture was principally a result of inveterate individualism and of the monition in the Second Amendment that the rights of the militia to be armed should not be infringed. But the individual liberties guaranteed under the Constitution did *not* include the individual's right to bear arms. Time and again that amendment had been held by the courts to mean that the Congress might not keep the *states* from maintaining well-regulated militia. Time and again the courts, citing the original intent of the amendment, had held that the right to bear arms was collective, not individual, and had to have ". . . some reasonable relationship to the preservation or efficiency of a well-regulated militia."

⊕

In its campaign to keep America armed, the NRA had frequently been supported by a number of conservation organizations, for the reason that a large part of the millions and millions of dollars collected annually by the states in return for hunting and fishing licenses was earmarked for conservation activities, for preservation of an environment in which animals and fish could live—for the hunt. If wildlife lived, the forest and field lived. It was a sound ecological argument. But would flora and fauna be diminished if wild men, known or potential —characterized as emotionally immature, thrill-bent, or criminally inclined—were denied guns? Probably not. There still were adequate numbers to keep conservation's cash-flow high, with license fees. There still remained an estimated sixteen million *law-abiding* citizens who used weapons for sport or recreation. The NRA, deep inside its building in Washington, had told the states and nation that it knew best—and had best interpreted—the mood of the nation and the meaning of the Constitution. And, for the most part, the Congress had heard the word. And played reverentially dead.

The first federal firearms-control legislation was enacted in 1934. Understandably, the Congress was alarmed by the violence of the twenties and early thirties, by bootlegging and gang warfare. The act required that those possessing machine guns, short-barreled and sawed-off rifles and shotguns, mufflers and silencers and concealable firearms (though not pistols) register these weapons and devices with the Treasury Department. The department would impose annual taxes on firearms manufacturers, importers, and dealers, and on the transfer of registered weapons and other equipment.

The NRA actively opposed this legislation. Its position was: "The issue is clean cut between the Attorney General and his undesirable law on the one side, and the sportsmen of America and other law-abiding citizens on the other side, with the armed criminals of the country on the side lines rooting for the Attorney General." To which Senator Royal S. Copeland responded: "A great deal of misinformation has been sent out over the country about the purposes of these bills. One would think from reading the records printed that it is the desire of the Senate to disarm good men and to furnish arms only to men who are bad."

The next national legislation was the Federal Firearms Act of 1938. This required the licensing of all manufacturers and dealers using the facilities of interstate or foreign commerce. It prohibited the knowing transportation of firearms in interstate commerce to, or receipt by, any person convicted of a felony, or any fugitive from justice. The law required that most kinds of firearms imported into or manufactured in the United States bear serial numbers, and it banned the interstate transportation of stolen firearms or those with mutilated serial numbers. The 1938 law also prohibited licensed manufacturers and dealers from transporting firearms into states in violation of state laws requiring a permit to purchase.

The next year—1939—the world was plunged into war. The question of firearms legislation all but disappeared, but in the postwar period the NRA returned to its traditional antilaw normalcy, declaring in 1948 in its official monthly journal, the *American Rifleman*:

The NRA headquarters can, and does, supply "medicine" in the form of a continuing array of arguments, facts and figures, through *Rifleman* editorials and special bulletins to members of the Association. Each member must consider himself as a local "doctor" who is responsible for curing the disease of gun ignorance by administering this "medicine" in convenient doses to his neighbors, local politicians and newspaper editors.

Taking "the bedrock stand that law-abiding Americans are constitutionally entitled to the ownership and legal use of firearms," the NRA asked "support of all loyal citizens who believe in the right to 'Keep and Bear Arms.'" In its battle to keep guns uncontrolled, the NRA went so far as to encourage "every reputable American who owns or shoots a gun" to join the National Rifle Association.

The word "reputable" stood out. The overwhelming majority of Americans, many of whom were weapons owners, favored controls. Public-opinion polls revealed that two-thirds and more of those interviewed wanted "a law which would require a person to obtain a police permit before he or she could buy a gun." When the same question was put only to firearms owners, a majority—56 per cent—advocated the same restriction.

But if the majority of Americans, including the majority of firearms owners, did not qualify as "reputable" because of their support of restraints, neither did some outstanding organizations that also knew there was a relationship between easy access to firearms and the prodigious gun toll in homicides, suicides, and accidents. The American Bar Association, the International Association of Chiefs of Police, the National Association of Citizens Crime Commissions favored controls. So did the media. Television networks had subtly and overtly editorialized for controls during documentaries on the gun traffic. *The New York Times* and *The Washington Post*, and magazines as varied as *Time*, the *Reader's Digest*, *McCall's*, the *Ladies' Home Journal*, the *Saturday Review*, and *Harper's*, had railed against our domestic-weapons lawlessness and had argued for strong national legislation.

Commonweal said of the NRA that it had "the megalomaniac conviction that its members are the only patriots and the sole sovereign power in this republic, and that any gun law whatsoever is treasonous, Communist, sacrilegious, and insulting, and to be thwarted by any means, even to ostensible cooperation with the law-makers, hypocrisy, and treachery."

In the fifties the executive committee of the NRA numbered less than two dozen, but effectively set and implemented policy for the nearly one million dues-paying members. In spite of its nonprofit status, the NRA had been able directly and indirectly to educate and influence legislators to its viewpoints.

As nonprofit organizations might lose their tax-exempt status by lobbying, the NRA, employing a convenient euphemism, "educated," instead. It "educated" by suggesting to its members, over and over again, the danger of riot-torn cities. In these cities, the appeal went, only one's own gun offered protection; the military, the National Guard, and the police would, no doubt, be terribly busy fighting off foreign enemies and/or domestic subversives. The NRA of course ignored the fact that few of its members live or had lived in riot-torn cities, but that most reside in rural, small-town, and small-city America. It also ignored this: even during the darkest moments after Pearl Harbor, when all able-bodied men were being called to serve their nation, when Japanese citizens were considered such a threat that in an action born of hysteria, and forever blemishing the American record, these citizens were rounded up and placed in concentration camps for the war's duration, even at so dark and hysterical a time the police were not denuded. Militia were not armed. The defense of the country was not given to the NRA or the man with the gun in his own home. Public safety was not in the private pistol.

But the NRA's emotionalism was best expressed in the first of the self-descriptive statements appearing monthly on the information page of the *American Rifleman*. There, without semblance of a blush, without a kind or knowing nod toward any other private or public institution in the United States, it was explained, quite simply, that the NRA was the "foremost guardian of the American tradition. . . ."

The argument of the NRA that licensing and registration provisions for handguns, rifles, and shotguns would disarm the public and thus render it easy prey for violent criminals, or to an invading or subversive enemy, was a blatant call to vigilantism. "Who then guards the doors of American homes from senseless savagery and pillaging?" asked an editorial in the *American Rifleman*. The answer: "The armed citizen represents a potential community stabilizer."

In fact, measures for regulation would have permitted householders and shopkeepers to continue to possess firearms. Licensing and registration for the legitimate user would merely have added a small measure of inconvenience to the largely unregulated mail-order and over-the-counter sales of firearms. It was this inconvenience that appeared to be the underlying reason for the opposition to legislation. Opponents said that registration would penalize the law-abiding citizen—who would comply—but not the criminal—who would not. The argument, accordingly, was that laws would fail to address themselves to the real problem of firearms misuse.

Yet, facts showed that most criminals purchased weapons through the mails or in retail stores, and did not often steal them. And facts showed that punishing the illegal use of firearms did not stop the crime from happening in the first instance. Watching the sources and recording the purchases, however, did provide an opportunity to limit access to those whose use of weapons was considered, by society, to be legitimate—the responsible and law-abiding collectors, hunters, sportsmen, and other gun enthusiasts.

Perhaps the NRA was more interested in the very substantial revenues obtained from manufacturers of guns in return for advertising space in the *American Rifleman* than in presenting facts to its members. Would a playing down of emotion and fear have caused advertisers to spurn their productive monthly opportunity, through advertising, to reach an enormous gun market? Would weapons companies have sold fewer weapons were registration required? Had Detroit sold fewer cars because drivers were licensed and automobiles were registered? It was like asking: would the television networks have lost audience if, say, instead of ten thousand dramatized murders annually, their police and detective programs had only half that number of killings? Would these programs have lost 50 per cent of their audience? Fifty per cent of their sponsorship? Not likely.

In all its years the National Rifle Association had found no criminologist of stature to support its arguments; no law-enforcement agency to back its stand; no outstanding police chief to advocate its claim; no psychiatrist to pursue dispassionately its emotional advocacy; no compelling body of legal opinion pleading its position. It stood alone, powerful if not prescient. It was a somewhat pathetic and questionable anachronism, founded before the frontier had disappeared, and unwilling to admit to change. Rifles and an enormous variety of shotguns were every bit as dangerous as handguns, accounting for about 30 per cent of the six thousand firearms homicides which occurred each year in the United States. What if the homicide rate in America was unmatched elsewhere in the world, including nations where—in spite of gun regulations—civil rights were untraduced? England gave the world the Magna Carta. And in England nobody was allowed to carry firearms at night; anybody wanting to hunt had to obtain a certificate from the local chief of police prior to purchasing a long gun; dealers were required to verify a buyer's certificate, register each and every transaction in weapons and ammunition, and record the serial number of each weapon sold and give the number to the police. And in the 1960s, in England the gun homicide rate was .05 per 100,000 population, while in the United States it was 2.7—about fifty times greater.

The geographic breakdown of gun murders also contradicted the NRA position that laws made no difference, that "when guns are outlawed [which *nobody* had suggested] only outlaws will have guns."

All of the states and the District of Columbia had gun control laws, and many local ordinances existed in towns, counties, villages, and cities. However, there was a wide diversity in the purpose and scope of these laws and ordinances. In the states with the most stringent laws (in the Northeast), about *half* as many gun murders occurred as in the Western, the North Central, and the Southern states. In a four-year period (1962–1965), the percentage of gun murders made an interesting, powerful, and persuasive comparison:

States having gun controls	Murders by gun as percentage of total murders
Massachusetts	35%
New Jersey	39%
New York	32%
Pennsylvania	43%

States having minimal or no controls	Murders by gun as percentage of total murders
New Mexico	64%
Arizona	66%
Montana	68%
Texas	69%
Nebraska	70%

Although the NRA worried over whether registration laws or controls would keep weapons from the law-abiding, it had not always shown such great concern over its own failure to screen members. The Association thereby unwittingly permitted weapons to fall into the hands of the lawless within its midst.

Straight shooting suffers neither lapse nor labyrinth. Not so bureaucracy. There were instances where recipients, affiliated with some of the gun clubs approved by the NRA under the civilian marksmanship program, were indicted by state grand juries for such crimes as conspiracy to commit murder, arson, the advocacy of criminal anarchy, and for substantive crimes under state law, such as the possession of rifles with intent to use them unlawfully. For example: the Jamaica Rifle and Pistol Club, chartered by the NRA as Club #7690, ordered and received from the Defense Department in 1967, four .22 caliber rifles, four .30 caliber M-1 carbines, plus two thousand rounds of ammunition; in actuality this club was the front for the "Revolutionary Action Movement" (RAM), a would-be terrorist group with the slogan "Kill, baby, kill."

Or, another example: eight of nineteen right-wing Minutemen arrested in 1967 on charges of unlawful possession of arms and conspiracy to commit arson, were—at the time of arrest—NRA members; they had received six thousand rounds of ammunition through the civilian marksmanship program; not long afterwards, the executive director of the NRA refused comment, in a public forum, on whether or not the national leader of the Minutemen, a life member of the NRA, was still a member—after being convicted of conspiracy and for violation of the Federal Firearms Act.

As with weapons generally, where the policy advocated by the NRA was aimed at maintaining ease of acquisition, and urged laws for punishing the wrongdoer—after the fact—the response to armed political groups was vague and ex post facto: "If we catch any of our members belonging to the Minutemen, Ku Klux Klan, Black Muslims, or any vigilante organization, they are put out immediately." Nothing said about the absence of effective premembership screening of NRA applicants; little—likewise—said about prepurchase screening of buyers of weapons. After all, there was a national confusion of federal, state, and local legislation concerning guns and their control. The Bill of Rights said nothing about self-control. It told of rights, not of responsibilities, reason, or restraint. Anybody could buy a gun to shoot with, without so much as a test for vision. The NRA could allow nothing to interfere with a profitable interpretation of the right to bear arms, or other derivative rights: The right to put distance between victim and assailant. The right to violence. The right to fascination, and to fear.

$$\oplus$$

In 1954 the Congress passed the Mutual Security Act. Section 414, "Munitions Control," authorized the President "to control, in furtherance of world peace and the security and foreign policy of the United States, the export and import of arms, ammunition, and implements of war. . . ." Under (b) of this section, persons engaged in such activities were required to register with the United States government and pay a registration fee. It was a simple matter of obtaining forms, responding to bureaucratic nomenclature, instructions, and definitions, and making remittance. If a person made the appropriate responses, he could be registered for a year for under one hundred dollars.

Although the Department of State and the Department of Defense were interested in the overseas destinations of arms, ammunition, and implements of war, and prohibited shipments to, or imports from, certain specified nations—principally of the Soviet bloc—on the whole there was a general and somewhat generous nonconcern. It was not the responsibility of the State Department to question integrity or purpose. Decency was assumed, mental capacity was unquestioned. If somebody, say the state of New York, wanted to bring forth evidence indicating that a prospective importer might be planning a revolution, such evidence could be advanced.

The Department of State was concerned with overseas, not domestic, outlets or utilizations. It was easier for a person to import one hundred thousand surplus rifles than to qualify in New York, under that state's Sullivan Law, for a pistol permit. What happened next door, as far as the State Department was concerned, was somebody else's business. The department had neither the authority nor the facilities and personnel to check the end use of imported weapons.

⊕

In early 1958 in Milan, General Vincenzo Muricchio, at the age of ninety-six, recalled his life and his direct and indirect involvements with the Carcano over more than half a century.

As a young artillery captain in the 1890s, Muricchio was assigned to the Officina Militare Pirotecnica (the Military Pyrotechnics Factory) in Bologna. There, in the metals laboratory, he struggled to control the explosive force of the new smokeless propellant which had replaced the black gunpowder of the earlier flint-lock years. Too often the brass cartridge shells cracked, causing the rifles to explode.

Muricchio described conditions: two thousand women worked in the factory; those assigned to the inspection of the cartridges labored in dimly illuminated areas, and therefore failed to notice small cracks. Muricchio smiled as he told of solving the problem by lining each lamp receptacle with metal polished to a mirrorlike finish. The then primitive and feeble electric lamps thus had their luminosity multiplied several times, and the women could see previously unnoticed imperfections and reject them as they came along. Most of them.

The general talked of other contributions he had made to the overall manufacture and use of the 91, of a scale he had designed to weigh the explosive cartridge charge, of his experiments with different metals for bullets, of the use of parabolic instead of uniform rifling for the barrel. He was proud of the testing procedures developed over the years at the four national arsenals, located in Turin, Brescia, Torre Annunziata, and Terni. Of the last he remarked that even in 1940, when Mussolini entered the war, and the pace and pressure of production accelerated, quality was never sacrificed. "In Terni," he said, "I saw rifles made that year that were among the best. The ministers in Rome wanted guns and more guns, but in Terni—the closest of the arms works to Rome—standards were not reduced. Mussolini gave us a national slogan, *'Vincere! E vinceremo!'* ["To win, and we shall win!"] but, as I told them in Terni when I visited there in 1940, to win you must have the best.

"Some idolize the machine gun. But when fighting

in the mountains it is not a question of firing a lot but of firing accurately." The old general half closed his eyes, as though trying to see, in the haze of a distance growing greater, a once familiar mountain pass. "It counts more to have a good sniper with a good ninety-one who knows the meaning of the motto, 'For each enemy a bullet, for each bullet an enemy.'"

General Muricchio recalled war after war, battle after battle. He recalled hearing news of bloody combat and disaster announced to three generations of Italian wives and mothers. He mused, "I am the last survivor of a group of military men who conceived an individual small-caliber rifle, accurate and easy to handle. . . ." Then, he appeared to grow tired and, leaning on his cane, went to a table near his bed. In a cardboard box the old general still kept some memorabilia. He took out a photograph cut from a newspaper. Against the shattered wall of an Albanian farm, an Italian soldier lay dead, his head resting on the stock of his 91.

From time to time the general examined that desolate picture. He thought he had known a boy like that. He wasn't sure any more. There were so many years of boys like that. That firearm which had served as the last pillow to a poor soldier without a name, without a face, far from his country, from his people, from his home, that was the same basic firearm which half a century and more ago, in the Officina Militare Pirotecnica, had given Muricchio frustration, preoccupation, hopes, and satisfactions. "You know," Muricchio exclaimed with a great sadness, "this campaign in which this boy was killed . . . those soldiers were good men. They had Carcanos supplied by the Terni arsenal. But sometimes the best is not enough. The Greeks were outnumbered and their equipment was inferior, but they were fighting in defense of their country—a cause they knew to be just. They counterattacked and virtually encircled us, one of the finest units in the Italian army, the 'Julia' Division. There were more than ten thousand casualties—dead, like this boy, or wounded—and five thousand were taken prisoner."

Muricchio looked out the window into the smog of a Milanese sky. "The boy in the photograph is ashes now. He trusted his gun. I wonder if he ever got to shoot it." The old general continued to stare into that dismal air, then turned and said, "Did I tell you it was a gun made in Terni in 1940? That was a good year for guns. I wonder if it is buried somewhere, like the boy." Then the wizened, weathered general, leaning his ninety-six years on his cane, hobbled back to his chair near the bed.

⊕

The Carcano was also receiving notice in the United States, though not in the form of nostalgia or reminiscences.

On May 13, 1958, Senator John F. Kennedy, of

Massachusetts, introduced a bill in Congress that would have prohibited the importation into the United States of "firearms manufactured for the Armed Forces of any country, or parts thereof for reassembly, except those which are curios or antiques or weapons of obsolete ignition incapable of using fixed cartridge or fixed shotgun shell."

The proposed legislation was supported by the Sporting Arms and Ammunition Manufacturers' Institute, for understandable cause. Many American gunmakers, including those in the senator's home state, were suffering from the growing importation of surplus foreign weapons that could be acquired for no more than the cost of a pair of shoes or a couple of tanks of gas. "So I think the bill," said the senator, "is in the interest of a great many jobbers, and at least one hundred twenty-five thousand retailers located in forty-eight states, and of particular importance to five arms manufacturers in Massachusetts."

The June 1958 issue of the *American Rifleman* carried a full-page advertisement listing a number of long guns and revolvers available on "easy credit" through the mails. One long gun was a "Late Model Mannlicher Carcano," made in Terni, Italy. The reader was warned: "Only 273 left." However, other Carcano rifles came to the American people—thousands and more thousands, the wandering waifs of wars. In chilling although not clairvoyant juxtaposition, on the other side of the page carrying the ad, the NRA proffered cursory comments on the pending legislation.

The NRA was careful not to "lobby," but it clearly was not in favor of restrictions such as those proposed by Senator Kennedy, suggesting that were such limitations enacted, preferential treatment would be accorded large manufacturers, while over-the-counter dealers would suffer. The NRA also made plain its position that restrictions on interstate shipments would impose hardships on those Americans in rural areas without easily available access to retail outlets. "Firearms legislation," the NRA contended, "is of insufficient value in the prevention of crime to justify the inevitable restrictions which such legislation places upon law-abiding citizens." Senator Russell Long, of Louisiana, would agree, arguing that legislation "might make it more difficult for murderers to get guns, but the man who intends to kill can always get a gun, no matter what we do." The senator did not go so far as to suggest eliminating laws against rape, murder, or the distribution of narcotics, simply because rapists rape and pushers foist drugs, notwithstanding the law.

⊕

On May 14, 1958, the House of Representatives debated an amendment to Section 414 (b) of the Mutual Security Act of 1954. In urging the House to adopt exactly the same language as found in the

Kennedy bill introduced in the Senate, Congressman Albert P. Morano, of Connecticut, said in part:

There were imported into this country in 1957 over one hundred thousand Carcano rifles, an 1891 rifle which was remodeled in 1938. Now, that rifle is not only an old rifle, but it is unsafe. There is no provision of law which requires an agency of the Government to examine the rifles before they come into the United States. Now, one hundred thousand of them have come in. . . . This Carcano rifle has been bought for seventy-nine cents by importers, brought into this country and sold to our sporting rifle shooters. . . . Let us find out where some of these Carcano rifles have gone.

The congressman was attacked by several of his colleagues who charged that his only purpose was "trying to help the arms manufacturing industry of his district." Congressman James Roosevelt, of California, argued that the central issue was whether the Congress would favor big industry as against the small businessman engaged in the sale of imports. Congressman Chet Holifield, also of California, charged that were the Morano language—actually the Kennedy language—adopted, "it [would] put ten thousand small businessmen and employees out of work throughout the United States." The imports, he carefully pointed out,

are bought and sold to the people of America who cannot afford one-hundred-fifty-dollar rifles. This means that the little fellow can buy himself a rifle and go hunting if he wants to. Later on, when the young fellow learns to shoot, and he has a cheap rifle, he graduates to a better one.

Would we stop the sale of used cars in the United States for the benefit of big cars? I do not think so, because we know that the fellow who buys a one-hundred-fifty-dollar used car eventually will buy a Cadillac. We know that the fellow who will buy a cheap rifle and go hunting, the young fellow who does not have a great deal of money will afterwards buy a better rifle. . . . The language in the bill is against the small businessman. It is against the young fellow who cannot put up one hundred fifty dollars to buy a new rifle. It is against ten thousand businessmen and their employees in America who take these rifles and remodel them for the people who cannot afford to buy new rifles.

The Morano amendment was defeated. The House instead adopted language proposed by Congressman Robert Sikes, of Florida, prohibiting "the *return* to the United States of any military arms or ammunition *furnished* to foreign governments by the United States under this [Mutual Security] Act or any other foreign-assistance program of the United States." (Emphasis added.)

By this action the door was held open to a continuing flood of inexpensive weapons from abroad. The estimated 50 to 200 million privately owned guns in the United States would be increased; the more than one hundred thousand gun outlets would be satisfied.

Fifty per cent of American households have at least one gun. Since 50 per cent of American hospital beds are occupied by the mentally ill, it is also accepted that millions of people walking the streets could benefit from psychiatric care. As though in recognition of this, and with no congressional inhibition mandated or likely, the catalogue of a New Jersey gun dealer advertised:

Achtung! Here is the acme of all German ordnance. The original Bazooka used by German troops to smash American-British forces all-over Europe. We have these weapons in two varieties. One is the standard Wehrmacht Model in regular olive drab color. The other is the camouflage color used by fanatical SS troops at the Battle of the Bulge. Both models are truly Germanic.

Congressman Sikes—whose language became law, permitting both Carcanos and cannons to enter the United States—was a life member of the NRA. Shortly after the House debate in November 1958, his daughter confessed shooting and wounding her sleeping husband after an early morning altercation. Next year, 1959, Sikes was given the American Gun Dealers' Leadership Award.

4.
The
Travels

The United States was ready.

As for the inefficient or nonserviceable Carcano rifles purchased in Italy, it was necessary that Adam Consolidated remedy their ills. A stranger to Italy, Adam again retained Alberto Bagnasco, who had served so well in the recently concluded negotiations with the Ministry of Defense. Bagnasco and Louis Feldsott would make appropriate arrangements in order that Crescent Firearms might live up to its promise to the hunters and target shooters of America.

The rifles required both work of substance and of cosmetics, a matter, essentially, of barrels and blemishes. To make the 91s acceptable to the American public, some would require shortened barrels, others a lengthening thereof; some would remain unchanged. Rust had to be removed; defective parts had to be replaced. The various identifying marks stamped on the breech and other parts of each gun had to be eliminated, and "Made In Italy"—in English—impressed. Finally, each rifle had to be test-fired.

Since the weapons were intended for hunters and target shooters, the alterations to the barrels were understandable. In heavy underbrush a short barrel has one great advantage: it is not easily caught or snared as the hunter weaves his way; if he has a sling and carries the weapon over his shoulder, such a barrel is less likely to catch a low-hanging branch. In more open country, for stalking deer, antelope, or black bear (all susceptible to the firing power of the 91), or for target shooting, however, a longer barrel is preferred because it traps the expanding gases behind the bullet for an additional infinitesimal moment, thus providing greater velocity and striking power.

Adam was to pay the Ministry of Defense for weapons (and bullets) as they were picked up from the Royal Arms Works in Terni, and Bagnasco was instrumental in working out details, with the knowledge of Feldsott, by which the pickups would be accomplished, the restoration achieved, and shipment to the United States realized.

As to restoration, Bagnasco made inquiry. A likely place would be Brescia, a city of one-quarter of a million people about three hundred miles north of Rome, an hour's drive from Milan.

Brescia had Roman law and citizenship as far back as 225 B.C., and has a superb range of churches, palaces, cloisters, fountains, and monuments built in the Middle Ages and the Renaissance—an era when it flourished by its manufacture of armor and arms for all of Europe. Here also are the Pietro Beretta Arms Plant, the gun works of Breda, and the gun works of Franchi. Although textiles are produced in quantity, and tourism is a growing industry in Brescia because of its proximity to lakes Maggiore, Garda, Iseo, and Como, arms and related tools of hunting and war are basic to this city. More so than with Terni, one is reminded of Undershaft's "Ask anybody in Europe."

There was Luciano Riva. His great-great-grandfather, his great-grandfather, his grandfather, his father, and he himself, all had worked in the gun industries of Brescia, a tradition of five generations uninterrupted even when his father started his own small business, making hunting rifles.

Riva himself never fired a gun in anger. In 1933, when he was sixteen, he served four months in the Italian army, and one day, while in the field with some of his fellow soldiers, looking for game to kill and cook, he saw a rabbit. He took aim with his 91 but could not pull the trigger. He does not remember thinking he might kill the animal but only that the sound of the rifle firing might frighten it. In any case, while he watched the rabbit through his sights, it suddenly darted away. With almost as much speed his own career in the army ended, not because he had been merciful but because the Fascist regime decided he would be more valuable, with his particular family tree, in the production of arms.

For two years he studied to become a technician and in 1935, at the age of eighteen, he was employed by the privately owned National Arms Works in Brescia to work on machine guns and 91s. Later, he worked for the Caproni Group of Industries, which bought the National Arms Works, where he helped to produce, as a head technician, some twelve thousand 91s each month. Still later, in the 1950s, he was offered a position as an executive with Breda, one of Brescia's major arms producers. His earnings would be more than adequate for his wife, his son, and his daughter.

It was not long afterward that Alberto Bagnasco, on behalf of Adam Consolidated and Crescent, journeyed north from Rome to Brescia, and approached Breda about entering into an agreement for the modification and restoration of the 91s Adam had contracted for. Such an undertaking, because of its nature and scope, was really not attractive to so large a company as Breda, and Riva was asked by the director of Breda what he would do if he were to alter some of the guns.

Breda then gave Riva six guns each of several different models of the 91 and told him to produce samples of his workmanship. "A very simple operation," Riva said: to shorten the 91s with long barrels, to lengthen those with short barrels (in either case by only a few centimeters), and to remove the markings and inscribe "Made In Italy" on each weapon—these were easy tasks. Shortening was a matter of sawing; lengthening was a matter of inserting a sleeve; the various impressions of digits and letters could be removed by grinding.

Having shown his results, Riva was visited by Bagnasco, was told of Adam Consolidated's pleasure with the samples produced, and was asked if he would undertake to contract for the modification of thousands of weapons. Riva replied that he had been asked to do this work through Breda and would not deal directly with Bagnasco and Feldsott, whereupon Bagnasco got in touch with the director of Breda, who in turn came to Riva. "Look," he said, "if you want to start a business of your own, sign a contract . . . go ahead . . . don't worry about us because we have quite a few other things to do." Ask anybody in Europe: to Breda, a contract of a few million lira or even more was inconsequential.

To Riva, the contract—those millions of lira—"constituted my blinders . . . immediate work which distracted me." Although it had been his hope one day to establish his own business for the manufacture of hunting rifles, Riva wondered whether this sudden contract was the proper foundation, something to justify a move out of employment and stability. But the "blinders" were greater than his resistance. And, furthermore, no specialized labor would be required. Had it been otherwise, he probably would not have gone ahead, for skilled labor in Brescia was at a premium, with the total labor market in the armaments field pretty much dominated by Beretta, Breda, and Franchi.

By contract dated May 24, 1960, between Adam and Riva, Riva was to repair, restore, and ship 150,000 guns, to be delivered to Adam Consolidated, in the United States, as follows: 50,000 guns by the end of July 1960; 15,000 in August; 45,000 in September; 40,000 in October. Riva was to be paid $1.50 per gun, a flat price regardless of the amount of work each weapon required. The cartons of parts purchased by Adam from the Ministry of Defense under its contract of December 19, 1959 (ten days before Crescent's incorporation in New York State), would be shipped to Brescia for Riva's use. When Riva picked up the guns in Terni, he was also to pick up ammunition; each group of finished guns, C2766 and its brothers, alike, was to be shipped to the States with cartridges in profusion.

At one point Adam had a meeting, attended by Riva, at the Ministry of Defense in Rome. "There were eighteen generals," said Riva, "who wanted to know from these Americans what they were going to use the guns for—they were afraid they might be sent to African tribes or to the Arabs."

Riva, too, wondered, but did not question. Knowing that in America anybody could purchase a semiautomatic weapon capable of digesting fifteen or more bullets at one feeding, "I could not picture to myself hunters or sportsmen using these guns because they would have to carry a box with the ammunition. The ninety-one holds only six bullets. And it would seem to me that people who are as wealthy as Americans and as used to comforts would not find it practical to walk around with this box full of cartridges."

In Brescia there was no place where Riva could do the restoration. Therefore, he bought an old factory in nearby Storo and had a fence erected around it so that once he commenced work it could be guarded, as was the custom, by the police. In the United States, however, Adam and Crescent had seen samples of Riva's work and were most anxious for the commencement of deliveries. As his newly acquired Storo factory was not ready, permission was obtained to complete work on the first eight thousand guns at the

Royal Arms Works in Terni. These guns, of course, came out of the supply warehoused there.

The weapons, repaired and restored, were dispatched to the United States. Words of satisfaction crossed the ocean, but no money. Riva was advised that the shipment had come with such rapidity that there was no time to transfer funds. The transfer, as it had been explained to Riva, was to occur through the Burkhardt and Company Bank in Essen, Germany; from Essen the transfer was to continue to the Banco di Roma. Riva was advised that Bagnasco, as Adam's agent with power of attorney, had the right to withdraw funds and pay them over to him.

Meanwhile, Riva paid his employees with his own savings and with bank loans. He also had to pay for the trucking of weapons, once the Storo facility was ready. He did not have to pay for the guns—these were part of the Adam contract with the Ministry of Defense. Having paid for weapons, Adam would advise Riva, through Bagnasco, and Riva would arrange to truck the weapons to Storo.

⊕

The first group of 8000 guns restored in Terni was part of an initial consignment of 25,000. The remaining 17,000, and then another 25,000, were trucked to Storo, and work on them was performed there in the facility Riva had purchased. By the end of October 1960, Riva had delivered 44,470 rifles to

Adam Consolidated. He had completed work on another 5502—for a total, thus far, of just under 50,000 weapons—but withheld shipping them because he had received only part payment, $28,069.50, much less than was due him.

Meanwhile, Adam was both receiving and giving criticism. The company was under pressure from the Ministry of Defense. Adam had stopped paying for or picking up weapons, and had advised the Ministry it could not take possession more rapidly than their restorer, Riva, could provide performance. Riva, who had done his best, with limited facilities and chiefly with his own funds, could render no more rapid service, nor could he even go further without full payment for work completed. Adam was claiming that Riva's work was not as it should be, that there were complaints from California and a complaint from Texas, where, it was stated, a gun had misfired, blowing up in the user's hands.

In short, the Ministry of Defense was threatening to sue Adam for defaulting on their contract; Adam was threatening Riva with a suit for nonfulfillment of their contract; and Riva was holding back on the final shipment of restored guns, in his possession, until he was paid in full what was owing to him.

Having received complaints from Adam, but never at any time any of the written documents, such as letters and reports, that Adam claimed to have received from various displeased customers, Riva went to Rome to talk with Bagnasco. Bagnasco said he could do nothing. Riva then cabled to New York to ask about the funds which Adam had promised and was contractually liable for, and received a return cable saying that funds had indeed been sent to the bank in Essen. Riva went to Essen and met with several bankers and was advised that the money had been sent to Rome. Riva apologized, saying he must have made a mistake and would return to Rome to obtain the money . . . because surely it was there.

He went to Rome and met again with Bagnasco, and now was advised that the funds were indeed in Rome, but that before payment could be made there would have to be shipment of the remaining 5502 rifles. Bagnasco said he was acting on Adam's instructions in withholding funds still due on the almost 45,000 rifles already received, and informed Riva that no funds would be released until all remaining weapons had been delivered to Adam.

Moreover, Riva was advised by Bagnasco that Adam had indicated that virtually all of the weapons were in a "deplorable condition." Riva could not believe this, even though it occurred to him that some weapons could have been damaged in transit; he decided to go to the United States. He was under pressure to pay his workers. He was out of guns to restore, for Adam had given him no more. He was out of steady employment, having left his position to go into business on the strength of the contract with

Adam. He was out of funds, having exhausted his savings. His borrowing power had ceased to exist. His credit was destroyed. He was in very serious trouble.

⊕

Riva arrived in New York City shortly before Christmas 1960. He was greeted by Irving Feldsott and with an interpreter along was taken on a tour of the city: Chinatown, Harlem, Little Italy. He was taken to Radio City Music Hall: "I have never seen anything to compare with it," he said. Then on to Yonkers and the offices and warehouse of the H and D Folsom Arms Company.

Riva was taken into a room where there were a number of cartons of rifles and thousands of rounds of ammunition. He was told that these were the rifles that were defective, and to demonstrate, an employee attempted without success to load a rifle. Riva objected, "I said to him that this rifle was not for hunting but was used during the war and that it loaded with a clip and if they did not know how to use it they should have let me know and I would have instructed some of their people in Brescia, and they could then have written an instruction sheet to go along with the rifle when it was sold."

Riva demonstrated the proper loading of the 91: the insertion of bullets in the clip, the loading of the rifle with the clip. He asked for several weapons, cleaned their barrels, inserted clips, and requested a place where he might shoot. He was shown such a place and made his demonstration. The weapons did not misfire. They did not explode. They worked.

While this was going on, the interpreter told Riva that he—Riva—did not understand the "American mentality." He did not understand that children "of eight or nine or even older would have their pockets full of money and that if they saw a gun in a shop they would go ahead and buy it and probably go around and shoot with it." Riva later said that when he heard this explanation of the American mentality, "I started getting scared that I might be held responsible for some lives, because these children and older did not know how to use these guns and would hurt themselves and hurt other people since they have a range of two thousand meters and more."

Riva spoke with Irving Feldsott and asked him what might be done about this and he, too, advised the Italian that he—Riva—"did not understand the United States, that America was not like Italy, and so on." Riva suggested that "we write to all the retailers and tell them either to recall the guns or to send out some instruction sheets." But Riva was admonished that this would be impossible: "It would take forever" was Feldsott's response.

$\oplus$

Riva was driven back to Manhattan and, left alone, decided to spend the day walking about. There was more sightseeing than sense to everything, he thought. He found New Yorkers friendly, and without difficulty was directed to Macy's. He saw a 91 in the window, priced at twenty-seven dollars.

On December 16 Riva had a meeting with the Adam people at their Fifth Avenue office. He recalls the date because of a great aviation disaster that occurred: A United Airlines DC-8 and a TWA Constellation, both headed for La Guardia Airport, collided above Staten Island. The Constellation limped a few miles and fell into the streets of Brooklyn. A boy, perhaps ten years old, sitting in the tail of the aircraft, survived, but only for a few hours. His lungs had been seared by the heat of the flames.

Himself under pressure to survive, Riva explained what had happened at Yonkers: that the guns were not defective, but that people did not know how to use them. Riva was told that the funds due him had been sent. He was glad to hear that he should not be concerned about the weapons because, in any event, they were cleaned and test-fired before being sold in the States. His expenses for travel to America would be reimbursed by Adam.

He was asked to sign a piece of paper, but his attorneys in Brescia had advised him "not to sign anything and not to make any decisions before consulting them," for he was alone "over there, whereas Adam had lawyers with them." So Riva indicated he would send his decisions from Brescia, and he returned to Rome on the first available flight.

⊕

From the Leonardo da Vinci Airport the ride into Rome takes, even without heavy traffic, close to an hour. To Riva it seemed forever. He went directly to the Banco di Roma "to make sure that the money had actually been sent, and I found that it had been sent and that Bagnasco had been notified of its arrival." But Riva, headed toward financial ruin, was not paid. About a month later, early in 1961, he was served with papers by the court—the Tribunale Civile di Roma—saying that he had not fulfilled the terms of his contract with Adam Consolidated. Adam was asking for the remaining 5502 rifles and whatever spare parts still remained, and demanding damages on the basis that Riva had failed to make his restorations at the pace called for in the contract, thereby preventing Adam from taking delivery of additional weapons from the Ministry of Defense, thus causing the company to lose out on part of the market for surplus weapons in the United States.

Riva retained an attorney in Rome. The attorney contacted Bagnasco. The attorney was advised that the litigation had been instituted because Riva had not delivered the 5502 guns. Of course, Riva had not delivered those guns because he was not being paid. Of course, he would not be paid because he had not delivered those guns.

It was a small, tight circle, particularly for a man such as Riva. He had never bargained for anything like this. And, meanwhile, Bagnasco was taking delivery of other guns, approximately eighty thousand in all, from the Ministry of Defense. He, as Adam's agent, had found another renovator. Aside from the almost forty-five thousand guns repaired and shipped by Riva from Storo, Adam, even with another eighty thousand 91s renovated elsewhere, still fell short of its contractual commitment with the Ministry of Defense.

The additional eighty thousand weapons were brought into the United States over the months ahead, up until October 1963. Adam was nourished; Crescent did business; Bagnasco was compensated. But Riva? He worked again for Breda, for only a short while. He took ill with diabetes and a circulatory disorder that painfully affected his legs, and was hospitalized.

At first Riva had had doubts about restoring the guns; he feared that they might be sent to Africa or to the Arabs. He was finally convinced that the 91s would be kept in America, largely for hunting. He had shortened some thirty thousand of the guns he had restored, making them more suitable to hunters for use in the forest and underbrush; he had lengthened some three thousand, making them more attractive to target shooters. The other seventeen thousand had not been changed.

Riva knew guns. His family had been gunmakers for five generations. He knew his work had not been defective, that his only failure, toward the end, had been in not removing the identification marks on the last of the guns, as with C2766.

Riva was only beginning to know that in the world of business there are paper bullets, proceedings troublesome and dangerous, though not as direct or fathomable as the barrel or projectile of a rifle. He would have much time to think. "It always happens that such things you realize after they happen rather than before."

Conditioned reflex? Although he tried not to relive the experience, he could not help thinking of Adam and Crescent and Bagnasco. From reflex and reason, from reason made reflexive by experience, he would say to those who asked, *"Mannaggia a me!"* Idiomatically, it translates: "May I be cursed!"; or "What a fool I was!"; or, most simply and sadly, "Damn me!"

$\oplus$

Riva made twelve shipments, all handled identically. At his workshop in Storo, the rifles were packed in the presence of Italian authorities. Each gun was greased as a protection against possible corrosion, then wrapped in a waxed or coated paper and inserted, along with nine other weapons, in a corrugated cardboard container. Packed ten to a carton, the serial number of each gun was checked and recorded on a slip headed, "Crescent Firearms, Inc., 2 West 37th Street, New York 18, New York." The slip also called for other information: the carton number, the model number, and the caliber. In the lower right-hand corner was the printed shipping-slip number. The slip was attached to the outside of each carton, and a copy was sent directly to Crescent, in New York. Adam Consolidated was the importer and, upon their arrival in the United States, had the guns stored in a bonded warehouse. Subsequently, before their reshipment to purchasers, they were cleared by Freedman & Slater Company, New York City, custom brokers.

The itinerary for the twelve shipments, like the packing, was identical and supervised. A trucking company, Fratelli Gondrand, would load the guns into a truck at Storo. The truck would travel south and west to Brescia, passing along the magnificent Lake Garda. Then, almost due south from Brescia to Cremona.

Then on again, the truck and the rifles, always preceded by two policemen on motorcycles, and always followed by two, for in Italy, the transport of weapons is not a frivolous matter. The escort would change in each province. From Cremona southwest to

Voghera, which is almost directly south of Milan; thence south to Tortona, and finally to Genoa, the greatest seaport in Italy.

⊕

The first shipment of Riva's reconditioned rifles was transported from Storo to the United States in the spring of 1960. The last of his twelve shipments to Adam left his plant, by truck, in September of that year. Crescent's Shipping Slip Number 3620 pertains to Carton Number 3376. The third-listed rifle of these Model 91/38s, all 6.5 millimeter, was C2766, made in Terni in 1940.

The paper work of cargo transport is prodigious; no mere snapshot and passport will do. Next comes a Bill of Lading, dated September 29, 1960, for the transport of "520 Cartons" aboard the motor ship *Elettra Fassio*, from Genoa to New York, "Freight Payable at Destination." The Bill of Lading indicates: "Address Arrival Notice To: Adam Consolidated Industries, Inc., 404 Fifth Avenue, New York 18, New York." Under a column, "Shipper's Description of Class and Contents of Packages," there appear the words, **"SAID TO CONTAIN,"** and below, this apparently innocent statement, "Obsolete Rifles." The rifles in the total shipment numbered 5200, of which 1700 were 91/38s and 3500 were 91s. The carrier, an Italian-flag vessel, was owned by Villain, Fassio e

Compagnia Internazionale di Genova, more collo-
quially known as Linea Fassio.

The motor ship *Elettra Fassio*, built in Genoa in
1957, had two sister ships, the *Angela Fassio*, built in
1956, and the *Carmela Fassio*, built in 1957. All three
were general cargo ships, diesel-powered, capable of
14.50 knots. All three were 447 feet in length, had a
breadth of 63 feet 8 inches. Each had a dead weight
tonnage of 3692 and a cargo-carrying capacity of
approximately 10,500 tons. Sleek looking, these motor
ships did not have the appearance of ponderous
ocean-going freighters. With low, streamlined smokestacks, each vessel looked more like an elongated
private yacht than a carrier of goods. Aboard the
Elettra Fassio, the 520 cartons of obsolete rifles, with
their "Shipper's Weight" of 20,800 kilos, did little to
displace water. At $.10 per kilo, the total cost for this
freight, collect, was $2080, or exactly $.40 for each
rifle to cross the Atlantic.

The next piece of pertinent information appears on
the letterhead of the freight-forwarders, Norton,
Lilly and Company, Incorporated, 26 Beaver Street,
New York 4, N.Y. It is dated October 10, 1960, and is
an advice to Adam Consolidated that "520 Cartons
Obsolete Rifles," weighing 20,800 kilos, which left
Genoa aboard the *Elettra Fassio*, shipped on Bill of

Lading Genoa Number 18, were "Due on or about" October 15.

Now comes a Warehouse Entry Form, Number 52737, dated October 24, 1960, from Freedman & Slater, the custom brokerage firm located at 8 Bridge Street, New York 4, N.Y. This advice, on U.S. Treasury Department Customs Form 7502, to Adam Consolidated, pertains to a shipment of "Five Hundred & Twenty Cts. Cont'g. Rifles Valued Not Over $5.00 Each As Surplus Italian Arms, As Sporting Goods." The advice indicates the guns have been placed in Harborside Terminal Warehouse, in Jersey City, New Jersey. All 520 cartons are accounted for. The date imported is given as October 17, 1960. Nineteen days for the *Elettra Fassio* to complete its trans-Atlantic voyage. The customs duty payable on this shipment of 5200 rifles came to $8494.50, or about $1.63 per gun.

The long log of the ocean crossing becomes complete with a memorandum, a Uniform Domestic Straight Bill of Lading, dated October 25, 1960, from Adam Consolidated Industries, Incorporated, pertaining to 520 cartons of rifles consigned to Harborside Terminal Company, Incorporated, 34 Exchange Place, Jersey City, New Jersey, via Waterfront Transfer Company, Custom House License Number 290, "In Bond Cargo."

The chain has many links: The city of Jersey City

was the original home of H and D Folsom Arms Company when it was founded in 1888.

⊕

Born in Terni in 1940, C2766 had had respite. It had become a creature of the indoors. Warehoused in Terni for fifteen years, from the end of the war until Adam moved it to Storo, it had seen little of the elements. Trucked to Genoa, bathed and coated in Cosmoline, it had been insulated from any sea air that might seep into the *Elettra Fassio*'s hold. Adam, which once had covered men's heads with hats, would for a while manage to keep a roof over C2766. At Harborside Terminal it now would remain warehoused for *two years and four months*. It rested and waited, but not at the pleasure of Adam or its customers—the United States Customs had impounded the shipment of which C2766 was a part. The customs office in New York City claimed the weapons had been undervalued so that the importer would pay a lower duty. C2766 rested and waited for twenty-eight months until an agreement was reached whereby additional duties, and penalties, were paid. Dollars at last brought it daylight.

By the time the Harborside Terminal Company received Riva's twelfth and final shipment of 91s, Adam Consolidated had already taken delivery, in the United States, of almost forty thousand rifles, shipped at various intervals from Storo, and successfully put on the open market through channels normal for the commercial exploitation and distribution of such hardware. Macy's was a customer; various large chains such as Sears Roebuck were included in the clientele. Wholesalers accounted for sales to sporting-goods stores, gun and hunting-supply stores, discount stores, and Army-and-Navy-surplus stores. Since the sales of arms such as the 91, for hunting or target shooting, was uncontrolled, the market was scattered and diverse. "Let us find out where some of these Carcano rifles have gone," Congressman Morano had pleaded in 1958, speaking of the first thousands of Carcanos to enter the United States. It was essentially the same desire as had been expressed in Milan by General Vincenzo Muricchio, just a few months earlier that year, thousands of miles away, although more out of raw wonderment than a sense of impending alarm.

$\oplus$

Periodically, Fred Rupp, RFD 2, Mink Road, Perkasie, Pennsylvania, picked up loads of 91s from Harborside Terminal. He brought them to his shop where, under a subcontract with Crescent Firearms, he would clean and test-fire each weapon, then ship it from his place to various customers designated to him by Crescent. If a carton was mutilated, he would repack the weapons in a new carton after cleaning and test-firing them. The new carton would be numbered by him with the same number as appeared on the original carton picked up from Harborside.

If a particular gun did not function properly, he would replace it with another, and he would indicate on the packing slip the serial number of the weapon removed and the weapon substituted. He would place one packing slip inside the carton, paste another on its outside, and send the remaining copies by mail to Crescent, in New York City. He himself kept no permanent record of serial numbers, but only of cartons shipped by him on Crescent's advice.

With Riva out of guns to work on and soon to be engaged in cross-suits with Adam concerning their alleged failure to pay him and his alleged failure to perform properly the restorations contracted for, with the Italian Ministry of Defense threatening Adam with litigation over its failure to accept more than 150,000 of the rifles contracted for, Fred Rupp—unaware that Bagnasco was arranging for more weapons—thought he was nearing the end of his supply when the *Elettra Fassio* disgorged her cargo on October 17, 1960. He would continue to service Crescent from the previous inventory; the additional 520 cartons, with their total of 5200 rifles, would move to the public as quickly as their availability could be advertised, their merits promulgated, their attractiveness assented to by purchasers in the most gun-given nation on earth.

The 91s continued to move out from Harborside, although more slowly than Crescent wished. In August 1962 Rupp signed at Harborside for one delivery against the account of Adam Consolidated. In October of that year he signed for four more deliveries. The supply was thinning, the inventory, not long after the final pickup in October, indicated a balance of only 86 cartons—860 91s out of tens of thousands imported, including the additional 80,000 restored, readied, and shipped independent of Riva under Bagnasco's subsequent arrangements.

Mr. Rupp's books showed that on February 12, 1963, on Crescent Firearms Order Number 3178, he turned over Carton Number 3376, containing C2766, to North Penn Transfer Company, Lansdale, Pennsylvania. His records did not indicate to whom this particular carton was consigned. In fact, it was headed for Chicago, to Klein's Sporting Goods, Incorporated, 4540 West Madison Street. Klein's had been founded in 1885; it was older than the 91 by six years, younger than the Royal Arms Works in Terni by ten.

Klein's six retail stores and its mail-order business offered a wide range of sporting goods and firearms. The firearms part accounted for approximately 25 per cent of the total sales volume of the entire operation. Fully 60 per cent of that firearms volume was in the field of mail order, generated by advertisements in Klein's own catalogues, and in magazines such as *Field and Stream, Outdoor Life, Sports Afield*, and the *American Rifleman.*

In 1963, the year C2766 left its Harborside incarceration of twenty-eight months, Klein's could, and did, advertise "Our 78th Year of Quality." Advertising nationally, this enterprise might also have boasted of quantity: Klein's was to the world of guns and hunting, to the target shooters and collectors, to the National Rifle Association members, and to the "Saturday Night Special" users, a major—and unregulated—arsenal.

The Rupp shipment on behalf of Crescent, via North Penn Transfer, was in response to Klein's Purchase Order Number 1243 to Crescent, dated January 24, 1963, for one hundred Mannlicher-Carcano rifles. At Crescent the record books indicate a sale to Klein's on Customer's Order Number 1243, consisting of "100 T-38 6.5 It. Rifles" at $8.50 each. This sales order shows that ten cases were shipped to Chicago, February 12, 1963, via Lifschultz Fast Freight, of Philadelphia, after transfer from North Penn. The weight of the ten cases was 750 pounds.

The cargo was carried in trailer number 43 operated by driver Jones, number 293 on the Lifschultz roster. Included on this same Chicago run were a variety of unspecified items, destined for Goldblatt's and Sears and Woolworth's. The 750 pounds of guns, including C2766, were checked into Klein's and signed for on the Lifschultz delivery receipt, above the printed acknowledgment, "Received the above merchandise in good condition." The date was February 21, 1963. It had cost $45.23, or $.45 each, for delivery of one hundred guns from Rupp to Klein's. On March 1, 1963, three weeks after Rupp had dispatched the guns from Perkasie to Chicago, Klein's issued check number 28966, in amount of $850.00, to Crescent Firearms. This transaction was complete, and another about to begin.

$$\oplus$$

Even before checking C2766 into its West Madison Street building on February 21, 1963, Klein's had begun to make known that this addition to its inventory might be purchased with the usual ease and expeditiousness that held old customers and attracted new. Klein's bought a full page ad in the February 1963 issue of the *American Rifleman*, published the first of the month, and read by an audience much larger than the National Rifle Association's membership of about 250,000. A white-on-black headline—the vitaminizing element to dubious bargain hunters—boldly proclaimed across the top of the page:

RECEIVED TOO LATE FOR HUNTING SEASON	Cash or Credit
Klein's Loss Is Your Gain!	NO
	Money Down
Save Now! But Hurry!	30 Day Free Trial

Two items advertised had nothing to do with firearms. Klein's was offering the "Famous Viscount Shortwave-AM-Marine Portable Radio" for $39.95, and the "Mayfair Brand 9 Transistor Walkie-Talkie" for $49.88. Apparent bastards among the bullets, the presence of these radios among rifles suggested to the reader that either the ad was inadvertently placed or that, more cynically, there was a hidden editorial message on a page devoted to guns: "We also have merchandise for those who would rather talk first."

On this page, for those who might aim better than articulate, however, was a listing that included:

U.S. Model 1917 30/06 Caliber Enfield Rifle	$29.88
DeLuxe Marlin 336C for 30/30 or .35 Remington	69.88
New Hi-Standard .22 Derringer Pistol, weighs only 11 oz. [shown in the palm of a hand]	29.95
Brand New! U.S. M1 .30 Caliber Carbine	78.88
Enfield Sporter .303 British Caliber	19.88
.38 S & W Enfield Pistol	12.98

And more! In unobtrusive type, appearing next to and under the pistol listings was the request: "Handgun Purchasers: Please send signed statement stating that you are 21 or over, not an alien, have not been convicted of a crime, not under indictment, not a fugitive or drug addict. Also send permit if your city or state requires." There was no request that this signed statement be sworn, notarized, or given any credibility beyond, or backing up, its claims or disclaimers. At the lower right-hand corner of the ad was a coupon, bearing instructions for both cash and credit customers, and having space for the purchaser to fill in his weapon preference, and his name and address.

Accompanied by a photograph—as were all weapons described—the third offering reading down the left-hand column of the full page was:

Late Issue! 6.5 Italian Carbine. Only 36″ overall, weighs only 5½ lbs. Shows only slight use, lightly oiled, test fired and head spaced, ready for shooting. Turned down bolt, thumb safety, 6-shot clip fed. Rear open sight. Fast loading and fast firing.

C20-T1196. Specially Priced	$12.88
C20-T750. Carbine with Brand New Good Quality 4X Scope—¾″ diameter, as illustrated	19.95
E20-T751. 6.5 mm Italian military ammo with free 6-shot clip, 108 rds.	7.50

Customers for all merchandise advertised were advised to add $1.50 per any size order, for postage and handling.

If the law did not require Klein's, or others among the nation's four hundred mail-order gun outlets, to be meticulous in obtaining the credentials and purposes of its customers, Klein's, at least, was methodical and thorough in its own housekeeping. C2766 had arrived on February 21, 1963. The carton in which it was shipped was opened the next day—Washington's Birthday—by Mitchell Scibor. He assigned a control number to each rifle and listed its serial number thereafter as each weapon was taken from the carton and checked for accuracy. Control Number 836 showed, from this point forward, a companion number, C2766.

On March 13, 1963, Klein's received a U.S. Postal Money Order, Number 2,202,130,462, obtained and airmailed the day before from out of state. The coupon enclosed requested Number C20-T750, the 91 advertised in the previous month's *American Rifleman*, with the four-power scope. The amount remitted was $21.45, covering the carbine and scope, at $19.95, plus the required $1.50 for postage and handling.

⊕

Klein's vice-president William Waldman, in describing this "package deal," substantiated the fact that the riflescope on C2766 was mounted before shipment to the customer and not shipped separately:

—Klein's catalogue number is the number for the described rifle with premounted sight;
—Had the rifle and riflescope been ordered as separate items, each would have been listed by separate catalogue numbers and would have been billed as such;

—The order for the rifle and riflescope was placed by a customer using a coupon clipped from a Klein's advertisement; the customer himself had specified the number of the "package deal";

—In order for the "package deal" to have been shipped with the riflescope unmounted, specific instructions of the customer would have had to appear on the order itself; no such instructions appeared.

The 91s, Mr. Waldman stated, were received without riflescopes, scope mounts, or without the receivers of the rifles having been drilled and tapped for such mounting. The rifles, accordingly, had to be drilled, tapped, and mounted with the riflescopes by Klein's personnel on Klein's premises.

Edward Stanislowski, a Klein's warehouseman and order clerk, said that upon receipt of orders for rifles with scopes it was one of his duties to see to it that the proper number of rifles and scopes were furnished to the gunsmith for mounting. After the mounting, Mr. Stanislowski would be required to match the guns with the particular orders and to see that they were turned over to the packing-and-shipping department.

William Sharp, a gunsmith at Klein's, indicated that he normally drills, taps, and mounts scopes on a group of rifles at one time, making for a more efficient operation than if the procedures were followed on a gun-by-gun basis.

Ray Lee Coleman, a packer at Klein's, readied C2766 for shipment. He initialed the order blank which Klein's had prepared, showing that the rifle, given Control Number 836 by shipping clerk Mitchell Scibor, had been dutifully mounted with a telescopic sight, manufactured in Japan, and obtained by Klein's from Ordnance Optics, Incorporated, Hollywood, California.

Ordnance Optic's owner, Martin Retting, possessed all importing and distributing rights to this sight, for the United States. Although his firm—he said—mounted the scope on the Argentine Mauser, the Swiss Schmidt-Rubin, and the British Enfield, it was his belief that Klein's was the only firm mounting this sight on the Mannlicher-Carcano.

⊕

It is indigenous to empire that men must be transferred, that hardship is a part of honor, that soldiering in the provinces must be endured for all its deracination. Hardware is treated more sensitively. It is carefully wrapped against the elements, guarded against dust and deterioration, and only rarely—not as with armies—indifferently transported. In America, humans cannot travel coast to coast by rail without changing trains. Not so with freight. People are hustled; goods are handled.

On March 20, 1963, C2766 began a new moving experience. It had traveled by truck and by ship, and been carried by hand. Now, in a cardboard carton about five feet long, marked "Fragile Handle With Care," shielded from the buffeting of transit by adequate layers of brown wrapping paper and newspaper stuffed to prevent shifting about within the carton, the parcel post rendered service.

In the seven days that elapsed between receipt at Klein's of the coupon and payment, and the parcel-post shipment of the completed order, Klein's book-keeping department proved itself as efficient as those others which had moved C2766 right along.

The $21.45 was deposited at the First National Bank of Chicago, on March 15. The total deposit that day to the Klein's account was $13,827.98. Only Klein's could say whether that was a good or bad day. It was, however, by the ancient Roman calendar, the Ides of March.

And, also on this Ides of March, the monthly newsletter, "On Target," published by the right-wing Minutemen, listed twenty members of Congress with whom the group disagreed. The list was surrounded by a black border with the words *In Memorium* (sic) above it. To compound the threat, the editors of the newsletter included a brief description of the Minutemen themselves: "These patriots are not going to let you take their freedom away from them. They have learned the silent knife, the strangler's cord, the target rifle that hits sparrows at 200 yards. Only their leaders restrain them. Traitors beware. Even now the crosshairs are on the back of your necks."

In 1963 the Minutemen claimed to have a membership of twenty-five thousand and openly admitted they held regularly scheduled guerrilla-training exercises. Their most valued possessions, guns and ammunition, could be hoarded with no trouble whatsoever. And, also with no trouble, they—or anybody else—could purchase bazookas, grenades, cannons, and guns in endless variety and in unlimited quantity.

With no questions asked.

Freed from the mummification it had endured most of its life, C2766 was traveling again. Many things would happen, much change would occur in the next few years.

In 1964 the *Elettra Fassio* and her sister ships, the *Carmela Fassio* and the *Angela Fassio*, would be sold by their parent company at a time when this concern found itself financially overextended and in need of cash. The purchaser was the Shipping Corporation of India, Limited, Bombay. The *Elettra* became the *Vishva Pratap*, the *Angela* became the *Vishva Kanti*, the *Carmela* was renamed the *Vishva Vir*.

In January 1966 Riva, burdened by debts, ill and

unemployed, was declared bankrupt by the Tribunale di Trento. He lost his home and property. His son Carlo became the support of the family and could not continue his education.

In 1968 the Tribunale Civile di Roma handed down its decision in the litigation begun seven years earlier, saying that Adam owed Riva the sum of $38,635.50 for the restorations he had done, for delivering guns *of whose workability*—these many years later—there *now* was indeed proof.

But Riva could not collect. Adam Consolidated by then was neither hats nor heads, had changed its name to Vanderbilt Tire and Rubber, and later to VTR, Incorporated, and resembled an amorphous amalgam, changing and shapeless, tired as an entity, torn as to purpose. Adam, in any case, was gone from Italy.

The Italian Ministry of Defense, its flickering fluorescents still playing off flaking paint, would deal no more in the Carcano. It had agreed to settle its contract with Adam for the $259,007.48 paid by Adam for guns picked up for restoration. It would not attempt to force Adam to take more of the rifles it had contracted for—a fruitless pursuit, in any case.

Alberto Bagnasco disappeared. In Sicily, where once he had been associated with the regional president, nobody had heard of or from him. The American

Embassy in Rome was able to report that according to its latest information he was not practicing law any place in Italy.

Books would continue to be written and published about World War II, but the young of the world were discrediting the battlefield as a solution to international disputes.

Italian soldiers would no longer harken to cannon, children would not be trained to war and killing. There would, in Italy, be no more "youth guns."

Terni was restored and transformed. By the mid-1960s it was a city of 130,000 people, still industrious, but in danger of losing their verdant valley to the ravages of pollution daily poisoning the air, spewing forth in pinks and yellows and greys and blacks from smokestacks large and small.

The Cascata delle Marmore was, at best, fancy plumbing—a gigantic faucet turned on and off by the heavy hand of man.

La vecchia puttana had changed. A whore no more, the Royal Arms Works was but a flirt, making no guns, fixing but a few. Even so, she might still take pride: in an experiment a Model 91 of her own, with sight modified to make it correspondent with a modern Garand rifle manufactured by Beretta, displayed a greater accuracy than the Garand.

But all this, these things, these changes, were yet to occur. It was still 1963. The gun, C2766, was in motion. It was leaving its plateau and climbing toward a peak.

5.
The
Triumph

In Dallas, Texas, the levee on either side of the Trinity River is about thirty-five feet high, providing a suitable abutment for people test-firing rifles—that is, if they chose not to practice at numerous local gun clubs providing target facilities to the public.

There were plenty of rifles around, said John Brinegar, owner of The Gun Shop. He even knew of the Carcano and declared that at the end of World War II, GIs began bringing the 6.5 rifles back to the United States, and that later, New York gun dealers began importing this rifle from Italy by "boat loads." It was a cheap rifle, in his judgment, and there was ammunition in abundance for it.

As to the rifle, as with the ammunition, there were

varying opinions. The manager of the H. P. White Laboratory, Bel Air, Maryland, had this to say: "Our many tests have shown that foreign military rifles are generally of good design and construction. . . . In a firing program undertaken by the laboratory, all rifles passed these abusive tests in a satisfactory manner; the failure of the Italian Mannlicher-Carcano . . . was due to the failure of the ammunition and not the rifle." It should be noted that in the tests Italian ammunition was used.

An agent of the FBI laboratory reported, as though in substantiation of the "firecracker" noise theory of "firing autograph" by which different weapons may be identified: "I have experienced the examination of Italian ammunition of various years of manufacture and of course, various makes, and I think it is of rather poor quality in this particular caliber [6.5], primarily due to the very short seating depth to which bullets are seated in the cartridge, which causes the bullets to loosen very readily in the cartridge even before they are loaded into a clip or fired."

The president of Interarms, the world's largest private wholesaler of ammunition and armaments, advised:

I think we could summarize our views by saying that we've had very good surplus Italian-made 6.5-mm cartridges and very bad ones; the latter we scrapped out as we test all lots before releasing them to the market. The quality of all surplus ammunition is obviously determined by the original production quality plus interim storage after production; in the past twenty years we've marketed about 35 million rounds of surplus 6.5-mm Italian cartridges all over the world. . . . I can show you 6.5-mm Italian cartridges produced in the 1930's which are better than those produced in the 1950's and, sometimes, by the same original arsenal. There's no rule of thumb. . . .

It's interesting to note that the Italian army NATO rifle team still uses the 6.5-mm M91 rifle in the NATO matches and still comes out in the top positions, it advises us, every year, against all other NATO teams with all other rifle types. It uses their own original 6.5-mm cartridges which are, now, at least ten years old minimum.

But the buyer of C2766 would possess bullets of special design—round-nosed, copper-alloy-jacketed bullets having a lead core, well seated in their cartridges, very accurate.

The Western Cartridge Company, East Alton, Illinois, a division of Olin Industries, had manufactured a large quantity of 6.5-millimeter bullets for use by U.S. allies still equipped with Mannlicher-Carcanos left over from the war years. When NATO forces adopted a uniform cartridge for new and improved weapons, millions of rounds made by Western Cartridge and shipped overseas were then found unnecessary and were returned to America. The Office of Munitions Control at the Department of State received a report from "an informant of unconfirmed reliability" that "in contravention of Section 414(b) of the Mutual Security Act of 1954, as amended," some of the ammunition returned to the States "was furnished to the Government of Greece under the Greek Aid Program in 1952 or 1953."

The informant said that the ammunition was sent from Greece to Canada sometime after February 1, 1962, and that two million rounds in one lot were brought into the United States and sold, although the law specifically stated there could be no resale of ammunition supplied to foreign governments by the United States under any foreign-assistance program. Transmitted throughout the country, these two million rounds turned up in surplus-gun shops, mail-order houses, and firearms stores.

John W. Sipes, deputy director of the Office of Munitions Control, and chief of the Arms Traffic Division, commented that "the informant's 'angle' on this is that for years the small arms dealers have been trying to get something done about transshipment of ammunition via Canada [by the large dealers and jobbers] to get around regulations which adversely affect their business." He explained that the United States "has an arrangement with Canada allowing importation of various armament items, providing that the items have been in Canada for at least one year. This latter condition seeks to eliminate, in part, shipments to Canada which [really] are intended for the United States."

Sipes also explained that a 1958 amendment to the Mutual Security Act of 1954 prohibited the *reimportation* of ammunition into the United States if this ammunition was originally sent to another country under the terms of any U.S. aid program. This was intended to protect American industry, although it did not go so far as certain legislators wanted. Before the amendment passed, attempts were made to ban the importation of arms manufactured for the armed forces of any country, *not* merely American weapons shipped to various allies. Sipes said that the Department of State would not take any action with regard to investigating the allegation of the informant. He advised that the department would definitely manifest its interest in doing whatever could be done to tighten up controls at the Canadian border with regard to ammunition importation, and probably would have conversations with other interested government agencies in this connection.

⊕

Neither ammunition nor a place to practice would pose problems to the purchaser of C2766, "A. Hidell," P.O. Box 2915, Dallas, Texas. And when he stripped away the wrapping and held the rifle in his hands and sighted through the scope, he must have felt a tingle of excitement and could hardly wait to insert cartridges and go to the Trinity River, or one of the gun clubs, to practice. For practice was needed. A couple of weeks later he took a shot at Major General Edwin A. Walker, United States Army, Resigned. He broke a window in the general's home, but missed his mark. It was April 10. It was Dallas. He told his wife about this episode; she warned him not to do a thing like that again.

He wouldn't need to tell her; there would be more practice and more familiarizing himself with the weapon and its telescopic sight, but no more practice at a live target. He had confidence in the gun and it gave him comfort. Although it had been made in 1940, he did not regard it as old: he had been born in 1939, just a year earlier.

This "A. Hidell" never knew his father, a collector of insurance premiums whose death, two months before the boy's birth, created immediate and substantial financial burdens for the family. When his mother went to work, the boy at first was cared for by babysitters, but at last it was necessary that he be placed in an orphans' home with his brother and half-brother. There he stayed for about a year until his mother, in anticipation of her remarriage, took them to Dallas. Then followed an interlude of apparent happiness for the boy, who for the first time had a father. But it soon ended, with his mother's divorce.

After this, the family increasingly felt financial pressures. The older brothers drifted away. When the mother worked as an insurance saleswoman, she often took the boy with her, frequently leaving him alone in the car while she transacted her business. When she worked during the school year, the boy had to leave an empty house in the morning, return to it for lunch and then again at night, his mother having trained him to do that rather than play with other children.

When he was thirteen, mother and boy moved to New York City. He was enrolled in a public school where children teased him about his "western" clothes and Texas accent. He began to stay away from school. Truancy charges were brought against him, alleging he was "beyond the control of his mother insofar as school attendance is concerned." He was remanded to Youth House, an institution in which children are kept for psychiatric observation or for detention pending court appearance or commitment to a child-caring or custodial training school.

The boy told his mother: "I want to get out of here. There are children in here who have killed people, and smoke. I want to get out." The chief psychiatrist at Youth House interviewed the boy, as did other members of the staff. The doctors and professionals concluded the boy was tense, withdrawn, evasive— one who intensely disliked talking about himself and his feelings. He was described as having a "vivid fantasy life, turning around topics of omnipotence and power, through which he tries to compensate for his present shortcomings and frustrations."

"I don't want a friend and I don't like to talk to

people," he admitted, openly. The chief psychiatrist concluded that there were no signs of psychotic mental changes, but that the boy had a "personality pattern disturbance with schizoid features and passive-aggressive tendencies." A social worker found him quite readily admitting imaginings about sometimes hurting and killing people. But the boy would not elaborate, contending such matters were his own business.

The chief psychiatrist reported the boy's mother did not understand that the youth's withdrawal was a form of "violent but silent protest against his neglect by her." The social worker ended her report by stating, "There are indications that he has suffered serious personality damage, but if he can receive help quickly this might be repaired to some extent." It was recommended that the boy be placed on probation on condition that help be sought through a child-guidance clinic where a male therapist might substitute for the lack of a father figure. The boy never received that help. Few social agencies even in New York City were equipped to provide the kind of intensive treatment required. Or it was simply a matter of overcrowding. The Community Service Society and the Salvation Army already had case loads too great. Returned to school, he was a severe disciplinary problem, and placement in a home for boys was considered by authorities, but before the court took action, boy and mother left New York City for New Orleans. There the boy finished ninth grade —an experience marked by classmates' teasing, this time over his *northern* accent. He quit school to work for a year, until he was old enough to enlist in the Marine Corps. He was seventeen.

In the Marines he kept much to himself. At the rifle range his practice scores were not very good, but when his company fired for a record, he scored two points above the level necessary to qualify as a "sharpshooter." To a fellow private he confided, "All the Marine Corps does is teach you to kill, and after you get out of the Marines you might be good gangsters."

He was shipped to Japan and acquired a girl friend. Some thought this gave him greater status in his own eyes. For whatever the reason, while in Japan he exhibited a new pugnacity, challenging one of his sergeants to a fight after a drink-spilling incident. A court-martial hearing found him guilty of wrongfully using "provoking words." The young Marine was now given a sentence of twenty-eight days in confinement; this partly canceled the suspension of a twenty-day sentence he had received in an earlier court-martial for possessing an unauthorized pistol with which he had accidentally shot himself.

In the Marine Corps he frequently baited officers by showing off his awareness of international affairs, and by quoting from books most of his superiors either had not read or had never heard of. He often expressed his sympathies for Marxism and the Soviet Union, and studied the Russian language.

Soon after returning from the Far East he was transferred at his own request from active duty to the Marine Corps Reserve, under honorable conditions. This was accomplished three months prior to his regularly scheduled discharge date, ostensibly so he might care for his mother, an accident victim. Almost immediately he left for Russia.

Despite a commitment to the Soviet Union, expressed with force and fervor in letters to his brother ("I never believed I would find more material advantages at *this* stage of development in the Soviet Union than I might of had in the U.S. . . . I always have considered this country to be my own"), he encountered disappointments. At the outset the Soviets told him he could not remain. The prompt response was an attempted suicide. His diary recorded, on October 21, 1959:

I am shocked!!! My Dreams! ***I have waited for 2 years to be accepted. My fondest dreams are shattered because of a petty official. ***I decide to end it. Soak wrist in cold water to numb the pain. Then slash my left wrist. Then plunge wrist into bathtub of hot water. ***Somewhere, a violin plays, as I watch my life whirl away. I think to myself, 'How easy to Die' and 'A Sweet Death', (to violins).

Discovered in time, he was taken to a hospital in Moscow and kept there until his recovery, ten days later.

Somehow strengthened in his resolve to remain in Russia, on October 31 he went to the American Embassy to renounce his citizenship. As a right he could have done so at once, but officials, considerate of his age, not wanting a young man of twenty to take so precipitous and final a step, discouraged him. They advised him to return in a few days. He never did. He was nevertheless permitted to remain in Russia.

A diary entry of August 1961, however, reflects considerable change in attitude and outlook: "As my Russian improves I become increasingly conscious of just what sort of a society I live in. Mass gymnastics, compulsory afterwork meeting . . . compulsory attendance at lectures. . . ."

And another, later diary entry: "I am starting to reconsider my desire about staying the work is drab the money I get has nowhere to be spent, No night clubs or bowling alleys no places of recreation except the trade union dances I have had enough."

Shortly thereafter, less than eighteen months after his defection, he began negotiations with the American Embassy in Moscow to prepare for his return to the United States.

While in Russia he married a nineteen-year-old Russian who had a diploma in pharmacy. Had he remained an expatriate for a longer time, he probably would have found it extremely difficult to return to the United States. But since he had tired of Russia rather quickly, U.S. officials, acting out of a conviction that it was better for America to bring a defector back home, presumably where he might be watched, assisted the couple to come to the United States.

The young man had first rejected capitalism, then communism, and now returned to capitalism. He wrote in his diary: "The Communist Party of the United States has betrayed itself! It has turned itself into the traditional lever of a foreign power to overthrow the government of the United States; not in the name of freedom or high ideals, but in servile conformity to the wishes of the Soviet Union and in anticipation of Soviet Russia's complete domination of the American continent."

Would he find happiness, someday, somewhere? His wife remarked, "Only on the moon, perhaps."

Back in America, he received an undesirable discharge from the Marine Corps Reserve because of his defection to the Soviet Union. He wrote to Secretary of the Navy John Connally (who shortly would resign and successfully campaign to become governor of Texas) that he would "employ all means to right this gross mistake or injustice."

He moved to New Orleans, became interested in the Fair Play for Cuba committee, and tried fruitlessly to obtain a visa to visit Cuba. He held jobs but found difficulty in working with fellow employees. He was fired from one position as a greaser and oiler of coffee-processing machines (he told his wife he was working as a commercial photographer) because his work was not satisfactory and because he spent too much time loitering in the garage next door, where he read hunting and shooting magazines.

His marriage—and by now he had two children—suffered difficulties, caused by the dual threat of economic insecurity and his continued frustrations and failures. He distributed Fair Play for Cuba committee handbills in downtown New Orleans and was arrested after a scuffle with three anti-Castro exiles. He was interviewed by the police and told them the reason he didn't want his family to learn English was his hate for America and his desire not to see them Americanized. At his own request he was interviewed by an agent of the FBI.

His Cuba interests and activities made it more difficult for him to obtain employment. He moved to Dallas and obtained work at the Texas School Book Depository. He was mostly alone; even his family was not intact. He had taken a furnished room for himself, while his wife and children lived with a divorced friend in nearby Irving, Texas. He visited them on weekends, except for the last weekend; his wife asked him not to come over because the divorced friend's former husband would be there for his daughter's birthday, and the two men did not get along.

On Monday, November 18, 1963, he called several

times, but his wife said she didn't want to talk with him again and hung up. He then arrived, unannounced, on Thursday, November 21. He told his wife he was lonely. He was not angry. He tried to please her, but she would not talk to him and he grew upset. He spent quite a bit of time putting away diapers. She asked him to buy her a washing machine because, with two children, it was too difficult to wash by hand. He said he would.

He asked his wife to come live with him in an apartment he would rent, but she refused, claiming it would be too expensive: it cost less for him to rent a room, and have the children and her live with a friend.

That night he went to bed before his wife. She did not speak to him when she joined him there, although she believed he was awake. Next morning he left for work before anyone else arose. For the first time he left his wedding ring behind, placing it in a cup atop the dresser. He took with him almost fourteen dollars, and a long object in brown wrapping paper.

Then came the Fire, and burnt the Staff
That beat the Dog,
That bit the Cat,
That ate the Kid,
That My Father bought,
For Two pieces of money.
   A Kid! A Kid!

The gun was twenty-three years old when it fired the bullet that streaked across 265 feet from the textbook warehouse in Dallas and blew out the front of the President's head. The National Rifle Association says: "Guns don't kill people. People kill people." But the assassin did it with a gun.

It was a long way, at least five thousand miles, and a long time, twenty-three years, from Terni, Italy, to Dallas, Texas. And who can say whether at *that* moment a sense of distance and of time, of history compressed, crept into the mind of "A. Hidell." It was his time, at last, to act upon the world. It was his time to find a place in history. It was his time to see whether practice had made perfect. It was his time to discover whether he could succeed at something. It was his time to find out how much steadiness and solidity he had absorbed, and now could call upon, from the Marine Corps boot training he had received as Lee Harvey Oswald. Denied much in life, he had at least this: under the weapons laws of Texas, possession of a rifle was denied to no one, regardless of background.

There would come a time when the vice-president of Klein's—the Chicago mail-order house—would tell, with tears in his eyes, and in a voice so choked he hardly could speak, how, late in November 1963, because of what happened, his company reversed its policy and began refusing to consign mail-order weapons to unknown persons with anonymous post-office boxes.

But tears in Texas come harder. Guns would remain supreme—no questions asked. No "who"; no "why." Several years later, another young man with a rifle climbed the campus tower of the University of Texas and, from this height, shot and killed fifteen persons plus one unborn baby, and left another thirty-three wounded.

⊕

President John F. Kennedy, in an address to the U.S. Marine Corps, Marine Barracks, Washington, D.C., July 12, 1962:

All of us, I am sure, ten years ago, thought that the need for the man with the rifle would be passing away from the scene in the nineteen-sixties. And it is true that there are a good many Americans tonight who are stationed underground in a hardened silo whose duty is to watch some tables and some dials and a button. But the very size and magnitude of these new great weapons have placed a new emphasis upon what we call rather strangely, conventional war, and they have made it even more mandatory than ever that we keep the man with the rifle.

⊕

Senator Roman Hruska, of Nebraska, from the 1967 Senate hearings on firearms legislation:

Conditions in New York are different from conditions in Nebraska or the Dakotas or Kansas or Colorado or

Wyoming, and that is the thing we can't get in our heads. In many areas there are less population than there were before, and the necessity not only for sporting purposes, but for just plain survival, sometimes against beasts, both two- and four-legged varieties, depends upon the ownership of guns.

⊕

Mad River Club, Pulaski, New York, from a document submitted to the 1967 Senate hearings:

Where is the rifle that has won and secured a Freedom for man that no other civilization has offered its people up to the present day? It is in the hands of "Ima Citizen." With it we have defeated the wild animal, the savage, and the enemy soldier. We have fed, clothed, and sheltered our families and have won liberty . . . with a gun. There are those who admit all this but say now all is secure . . . and we have our freedom; because of this you can't have a gun for legitimate use because you might get hurt, or a criminal might get it and commit a crime. Well . . . thanks a lot! We are going to stand and fight for the unrestricted sporting arms as long as we remain honest citizens and as specified by the Bill of Rights. . . .

The idea of reducing crime by registering guns is just an excuse for added taxes. . . . Registration would create another government bureaucracy and money would be needed to run it. Registration would become so expensive that no one could afford to own a gun legally. Perhaps the wish is to make gun ownership so expensive that only the rich can afford it, and gradually by continually increasing taxes and fees, the people of these United States will be reduced to a European or Asiatic type peasant . . . we hope not! . . .

We beg you to allow us the Freedom to bear arms and to

use them to protect ourselves from crime and criminals, from any despot, tyrant, conspirator, or foreign power which if we were disarmed would try to subject us to dictatorship or worse. . . .

. . . right or wrong, my country. . . . What a height of emotion this is . . . demonstrating a complete love, honor, and respect for one's homeland. We subscribe to this 100%. . . .

It is not the gun that commits the crime, it is the greedy, warped, rapacious mind that uses it as a tool for unlawful deeds. . . .

$$\oplus$$

From the 1967 Senate hearings:

COMMITTEE STAFF: Could you tell us what the chief objection is to the registration of firearms?

CONGRESSMAN ROBERT SIKES [of Florida]: Well, I think that recent history will show us that when the Germans invaded the Scandinavian countries, they found a registration of weapons to be an extremely useful thing. They knew exactly where to go, they had the lists, they knew exactly where to go to pick up all the weapons. This helped curb resistance. . . . We have spot insurrections going on in the United States. Well suppose that spreads? Suppose that same crowd decided to take over Washington? . . . That kind of people would want a registration of the weapons in this country in order to stamp out whatever resistance there might be before it could become effective. . . . What is the reason for having registration of firearms? . . . Why should the Federal Government go to the expense of maintaining these records . . . building new buildings to file them in. . . . I think it is the kind of thing that runs counter to the grain of Americans who are accustomed to enjoying some freedom, not to be harassed at every turn by a new brand of bureaucracy.

⊕

From documents inserted in the hearings record by Senator Strom Thurmond, of South Carolina, illustrating the Marine Corps philosophy as to long-range sharpshooting, and in support of the civilian-marksmanship program established by Congress:

As the late NRA Executive Director, Maj. Gen. Merritt A. Edson, USMC (Ret.), said in an editorial in the *American Rifleman* in 1951: "It is not my intent to imply that the ability to shoot straight is the beginning and the end of national security. But it is that part of national security which affects the individual more than any other."

⊕

And, in the last hours of his life, on the morning of November 22, 1963, President Kennedy remarked to Kenneth O'Donnell and to Mrs. Kennedy that ". . . if anybody really wants to shoot the President it is not a very difficult job—all one has to do is get on a high building someday with a telescopic rifle, and there is nothing anybody can do to defend against such an attempt."

⊕

A fellow employee encountered Lee Harvey Oswald:

He asked me what were the people gathering around on the corner for and I told him that the President was supposed to pass that morning, and he asked me did I know which way he was coming, and I told him, yes, he would probably come down Main and turn on Houston and then back again on Elm. Then he said, "Oh, I see," and that was all.

The assassin juggled the weapon to get the feel of its balance. It was a good length: 40.2 inches. It had a good weight: 8 pounds, even.

He took his position at the sixth-floor window of the orange brick Texas School Book Depository warehouse. In Terni, the sun already had set on the yellowish-orange stucco walls of the Royal Arms Works.

It was November 22, 1963. Politics—the need to keep Texas a "safe" state for the Democrats—had sent the young President afield. He had barely carried the vote there in 1960, and now there was bitter in-fighting by and between party regulars and dissidents.

⊕

In mid-town New York City, Sandy Richardson, who would think of the firecracker sound, was sitting down to lunch. Downtown, a New York State Joint Legislative Committee was meeting at 270 Broadway to discuss better control of long guns. *But only for New York State.* It still was each state for itself.

⊕

An expert later said what any marksman knew:

This is a definite advantage to the shooter, the vehicle moving directly away from him and the downgrade of the street, and he being in an elevated position made an almost stationary target. . . . Using the scope, rapidly working the bolt and using the scope to relocate your target quickly, and at the same time when you locate that target you identify it and the cross hairs are in close relationship to the point you want to shoot at, it takes just a minor move in aiming to bring the cross hairs to bear, and then it is a quick squeeze.

The time would not be long; it was down to minutes. Not the gun's twenty-three years, not the assassin's twenty-four.

Crowds cheered as the Presidential motorcade drove through the city. Governor John Connally's wife, riding in the limousine with her husband, the President, and his wife, said, "Mr. President, you can't say Dallas doesn't love you."

And then it was half past noon.

In five seconds three shots were fired. One missed. The first that hit the President entered in the lower back of his neck and emerged at the lower front. He grabbed at his throat.

And then the shot that killed was fired. Mrs. Kennedy saw the President's skull torn open. "Oh, my God—" she cried out.

A life was ended:

The body is that of a muscular, well developed and well nourished adult Caucasian male measuring 72½ inches and weighing approximately 170 pounds. . . . There is beginning rigor mortis. . . . The hair is reddish brown and abundant, the eyes are blue. . . .

The career of C2766 was over.